D1058605

Also by Dennis Covington

Lizard
Lasso the Moon
Salvation on Sand Mountain

Also by Vicki Covington

Gathering Home
Bird of Paradise
Night Ride Home
The Last Hotel for Women

cleaving

cleaving

the story of a marriage

dennis and vicki covington

north point press

farrar, straus and giroux

new york

North Point Press
A division of Farrar, Straus and Giroux
19 Union Square West, New York 10003

Copyright © 1999 by Dennis and Vicki Covington
All rights reserved
Distributed in Canada by Douglas & McIntyre Ltd.
Printed in the United States of America
Designed by Jonathan D. Lippincott
First edition, 1999

Library of Congress Cataloging-in-Publication Data

Covington, Dennis.
    Cleaving : the story of a marriage / Dennis and Vicki Covington.
      p.   cm.
    ISBN 0-86547-548-2
    1. Covington, Vicki—Marriage.   2. Covington, Dennis—Marriage.
3. Women novelists, American—20th century—Biography.   4. Married
people—United States—Biography.   5. Journalists—United States—
Biography.   I. Covington, Vicki.   II. Title.
PS3553.0883Z64   1999
813'.54—dc21
[B]   98-51173

The names of some individuals, along with identifying details, have been changed
to protect their privacy.

contents

Therefore shall a man leave his father and his mother, and shall cleave unto his wife: and they shall be one flesh.

—Genesis 2:24

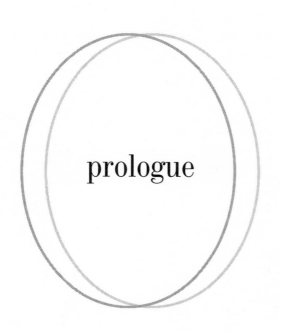

prologue

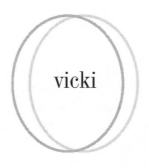

vicki

On a Tuesday night in January 1997, a woman appeared in
the foyer of my house. She'd walked in without knocking.
She had wild and beautiful dark curls. She was waving a handful of letters. "You're fucking my husband," she spit.

I made her go outside.

I did this because one of my daughters was standing nearby.
I knew the person. Her name was Kira. Her eyes, that night,
were demonic. I swear the irises were red.

"That's not true," I told her, "and I can pass a polygraph."
I meant it, although it was also true that I'd written the letters
she was holding, and they were addressed to her husband.

The word *polygraph* did what it was supposed to do. She
shut up long enough for me to say, "You can do to me
whatever you want, just don't hurt my children."

This conversation occurred in my front yard—on a nice
lawn, manicured monthly by a landscape service. In summer,
the grass is verdant. I plant orange impatiens to border the
shrubs. I plant pansies by the mailbox. I don't water any of

it, though, and sometimes things start to die. My neighbors forgive my inept gardening. They forgive the whiff of white trashiness they occasionally sniff in us, the way boards and pipes and newspapers and trinkets accumulate on our porch, the way women arrive at night with papers in hand, screaming, "You're fucking my husband."

We live on a cul-de-sac. As a mother, I have a twofold purpose on the street. I let kids dance on the tables, and I bury dead animals in the side yard. I've buried frogs, lizards, chipmunks, butterflies, rats, birds, and a golden retriever. I like pet funerals. They make me feel worthwhile. I always say a prayer with the kids. They never close their eyes or look at the earth. They peer up at me. Perhaps they're looking for signs of phoniness, or maybe they're just taking a mental snapshot to file in their internal scrapbooks.

I wonder if the neighborhood kids were drifting off to sleep the night Kira was waving the letters in my face. I wonder if they heard my voice saying "Polygraph."

There are a lot of ways to get the truth out of somebody. The lie detector is one. Torture is another. Hypnosis. Cross-examination. Asking the right questions—as skilled journalists, therapists, attorneys, and investigators are able to do.

Most of the time people want to talk. Southerners find it satisfying in the way that overindulgence in anything is satisfying, and they'll tell you more than you want to know. They love a story even when the truth contained therein wrecks their reputation and sets fire to things. For the writer, the truth is harder to find. Before I knew anything about well-drilling, I used to think that hitting water meant tapping into a flowing, underground river. I didn't know that you get to water by gradually coming to the place where saturation has occurred, and that this layer of earth is called an aquifer. I didn't know that water, like truth, craves release from whatever is holding it back. When you drive a well, you are relieving pressure. So pure truth, like pure water, comes not under pressure but when the pressure is taken away. You can submit to oath or torture or lie detectors, as many do. But it won't be as pure as the truth that comes from the well you've driven into yourself.

Dennis convinced me that you can drill a well by yourself. A hand auger is all you need. You rotate the handle the same way you turned the handle of your grandmother's old eggbeater.

The first water you come to, if you auger down far enough, isn't the water you want. It's surface water. The good water is four to twelve feet deeper. To get this water you have to drive a well point. Water, like truth, wants to be freed from its hiding place. It wants to come up. It will rise.

A couple of days after Kira came over, I went to talk to a polygrapher; I'll call him Grady. Grady knew I was a writer, and he said, "You need this information for a novel?" He was a calm, scrupulous man with degrees in law and counseling, somebody who didn't intimidate, despite his job.

"No," I told him, as we stood by the polygraph instrument, a big brass plate with wires, set down in a desk well, which administers what is formally known as a "forensic psycho-physiological detection test." I told him I was writing a memoir of my marriage. I told him I wanted to be hooked up—not to be questioned, but to sit in the big black chair. He was very accommodating. He put the pneumograph tubes over my chest to monitor and record movement in my thoracic cavity. He attached finger plates to monitor and record galvanic skin response. "Sweating," he noted. Finally, he put the cardio cuff on my arm to monitor and record changes in heart rate and blood pressure.

I stared at the wall.

I was wearing a blue sweater, a white turtleneck, and a T-shirt.

"You've really got on too many layers of clothes," Grady said. "If we were actually questioning you, this wouldn't be accurate."

He told me that I would—if this were real—be asked to keep my eyes open, find a spot on the wall, and focus. I did this anyway.

"Now what?" I asked him. It struck me that some people might start crying at this juncture, and I asked him if this was so. He said yes, it had occurred. I almost started crying then, myself, because I realized why I was there.

"See," I told him. "The writer is in the big black chair. The reader is the polygrapher. The reader is going to know when the needle flutters. The reader is going to know when I'm lying. Do you understand?"

"Not really," he said. Then he smiled, as if to say, "Dispense with the metaphors."

But I was all strapped up, focused on the spot on the wall. I waited for him to say something. "The instrument doesn't differentiate big lies from little lies. A lie is a lie," Grady told me.

I looked at the Velcro on the finger plates. "My nails are fake," I told him. "They're acrylic." He smiled, shrugged.

If this were real, he told me, he'd adjust all the knobs to bring the instrument into balance with my personal physiology. Then he'd ask me to make any last-minute movements. "Most people start to itch," he noted.

"Or cough," I said.

"Yes," Grady affirmed.

We'd gone as far as we were going to go. He unstrapped me, and I stood by the instrument. I stared at the big black chair. I knew that even though I was free to go, I'd return, in my mind, to this room whenever I sat down to write this book, to see if my body might be reacting to the stress of lying. Fight, flee, or freeze?

The writer better freeze. There are questions to be answered. Like the one Kira asked me in her kitchen the morning after the incident in my yard. I'd told her that Dennis knew about the relationship I'd been having with her husband, and she'd looked at me incredulously.

"What kind of marriage is that?"

The poet W. H. Auden says, "Tell me the truth about love."

I hope we can.

Kira's husband called me the morning after his wife appeared at my door, screaming. He asked if I would come over. He and Kira wanted to talk to me. I wanted to go, I'm not sure why. I threw on some jeans. They live in a nice place, set back from the road. I parked in the driveway. It was raining hard. Kira's husband let me in. We walked through the garage, up carpeted stairs to the kitchen. They had a new floor.

It was sparkling, but Kira was dabbing up a spot with a wash-cloth.

"Chocolate milk," she said, and I knew I'd always remember her saying this. I knew I'd remember it in the way people remember insignificant details about a car wreck.

We sat at their kitchen table, the three of us.

"How long?" she asked, cutting me in two with her eyes.

I wanted to make a big deal out of the fact that we hadn't done it. I wanted to justify it. I wanted to say, "Look, my mother has Alzheimer's and my daddy has Parkinson's disease, and I'm taking care of them, and I'm forty-four, and your husband is older than me and he came along at a vulnerable moment and I latched on to him like a leech." But she had her chin up. Her eyes were unyielding. It crossed my mind that she was gorgeous.

"How long?" she asked again.

"A few months," I told her.

The rain had picked up. My daughter, Laura, is afraid of storms. She's also psychic, like her grandmother. Once, I popped an ivory-colored balloon while I was cleaning up her bedroom because I was tired of looking at it. When I picked her up at school, she was crying. "Why did you do it?" she asked. "Why did you pop it?" I felt horrible, horrible and caught, just like I was feeling now.

"Did you really think this would work?" Kira asked, her eyes augering deep.

I studied her.

"Who did you think you were fooling?"

I didn't know what to say.

"You tried to seduce him with *words*," she said, gesturing at him with the letters. I tried not to look over at him.

"I'm going to sue you for alienation of affection," she said.

I didn't know what this meant. "I don't have any money," I told her, and this was true. We'd already spent the first part of the advance for the book to get ourselves out of debt.

"It's not a civil suit," she said. "Your name will just be on my divorce papers." I thought of judges. Alabama's secretary of state is my neighbor. I wondered if he'd find out.

I think Kira's table was made of wood, the walls a dark red. The window was directly in front of me. Kira looked at me, then at her husband, and finally she pulled out the big guns. "So you're a deacon in your church," she said.

I felt myself disappearing.

"What are you going to do? Keep standing up there, reading your Scripture? You're going to have to account for what you do someday," she said, and I noticed that her nails were a natural color. They weren't fake like mine.

"God isn't mean," I said to her. I meant it. Even though I'd wronged her, I meant this.

"Maybe you don't belong in a Baptist church," she said. Her eyes were on fire again.

"No, I probably should be Episcopal," I replied.

"Dennis knows about this?" she demanded.

"Yes," I told her.

"What kind of marriage is that?" Her eyes widened, and I tried to decide if they were blue or green. I knew that her favorite drink was a Rusty Nail. He'd told me.

"We just figured there would be things like this, along the way," I said.

"Like what?"

"You know, you'll be attracted to other people. You'll try to not act on it, and I didn't for all these years. Then sometimes you walk in deeper than you meant to. This is life."

The word *life* incensed her. "No," she said, "no, this isn't life, Vicki. You don't have to get involved. You can choose to be faithful to your husband, like I have." I knew that she hadn't been faithful to her first husband. Her current marriage had begun in an affair. I knew she was capable of deceit. But I didn't bring this up. She had me.

The strange thing is that I didn't want to leave. Even when we had all stopped talking and I knew it was time to go, I tarried. I toyed with the drawstring of my blue windbreaker. I took a sip of water. Kira and her husband were drilling holes in one another with their eyes. "There's a lot we need to talk about now," she said, without looking at me. "Just us," she said evenly, and I knew then that I had to go.

"If you see him again, I'll do something to hurt you," she said.

"What will you do?" I wanted her to say it out loud. I wanted him to witness it.

Her eyes traveled from me to him, back to me. "I'll either hurt you physically or I'll do something to make your life unbearable."

Right before we got up from the table, Kira's husband gave a brief sermon on forgiveness, which surprised me, since he's not prone to religiosity. Then we all rose. I took a wrong turn, and they had to steer me correctly. We started toward ground level, and that's when I lost it. I lost it because photographs of all their children were hanging along the stairwell.

I caught glimpses of the straw-colored gymnasium floor, the baseball fields, the friends, weddings, family vacations, the faces of their children giving it all to the camera or to the sporting event at hand. When we got to the bottom of the stairs, I turned abruptly. I was in her face.

"I'm sorry," I told her.

"I haven't cried yet, and I don't want to do it now," she said.

I wanted to hug her. "Can I touch you?" I asked.

"*No*," she whispered, and the word was ripe.

I turned for the door. It was raining cats and dogs. He asked me if I wanted an umbrella. I didn't. I wanted to make a dash for it. I backed the car up into the street. I drove home, and on the way home I didn't turn the radio on. I didn't think anything. When I got home, Dennis was in the living room drinking a cup of coffee.

We live in a house we can't afford, in a neighborhood we can't afford, in a life we can't afford. Our neighbors are lawyers, CPAs, stockbrokers. Our place is modest, I suppose, by middle-class standards—three bedrooms, two baths. But we're writers, and we can't always pay the bills. We don't manage money well. We give a tenth of our writing money to the church, though. We always write the tithe check, right when an advance comes in. We do it in the same way we charge plane tickets on Amex or put Christmas on Visa. We do it without thinking. We do most everything without thinking. I'm not sure we know how to think. We're impulsive—both of us.

Dennis was on the loveseat that morning.

"I'm in a mess," I told him.

He leaned forward, cradling his mug. I sat on the couch. It's made of ivory material, with rose and blue lines. The walls are gray. The entire living room is minimalist, monochromatic, like a black-and-white photograph, a documentary of what might be.

We talked about Kira spreading the news.

"The letters," I said to Dennis.

He looked at me.

"They made everything seem more than it was. You know, I wrote it up better than it happened. You know," I said, hoping he'd know.

Dennis noted that no newspaper would print them, and this was a comforting thought, especially since I used to do an editorial slice-of-life column for *The Birmingham News*. I knew Dennis was mad at me, though. We'd tried to give each other freedom in all things, and he was getting burned for this one. We'd had a big fight a few months back about my relationship with Kira's husband, but he'd let it go, not asking any more questions, figuring, I suppose, that it would play itself out. Plus, he'd had his own dances over the years. But whatever irritation or anger he was feeling, he was, I could tell, mostly worried about me. I saw it in his eyes. He was siding with me the way people side with a family member who's been arrested.

"The book," I sighed.

This was a painful topic lately, anyway. In light of the current event, the book we'd planned to write about our marriage seemed virtually out of the question. Here was the intended starting point: A couple of recovering alcoholics with two miracle children and dual careers, happily settled in the suburbs. The couple had held on to their sobriety and their passion for one another, but were still vaguely unhappy and unfulfilled. Love had not been enough. Work had not been enough. There was something else we were longing for. We called it "living water," because that's the phrase Jesus had used to describe the abundant life he was offering the Samaritan woman at the well.

So we'd turned the metaphorical into the actual and trained ourselves to hand-drill wells so that we could bring clean water to places that didn't have any, redeeming ourselves and our marriage by simple Christian service. That had been the concept, anyway.

A few nights later, Dennis came in from teaching with light in his eyes. "I've got it," he said. "I've got a radical idea. I know where you can begin the book."

I looked at him, hopeful.

"It begins on a Tuesday night in January 1997, when a woman comes to the front door waving a batch of letters in your face."

I felt the hairs stand up on my arms. Dennis is a journalist, and he believes in reporting the truth. He believes you can be an unethical person and still be an ethical writer.

"I can't do that," I said, but my eyes were wide open, and I knew that he saw that I could.

A few weeks later, I sit here typing this. I'm typing it from a loft we rent and can't afford. We don't live here; we just write here. In winter, the bare trees allow a view of the apartments, homes, and condos sprinkled along the slope of Red

Mountain. Birmingham lies in a valley, and this particular neighborhood is called Five Points South. It's not a place for raising children, but it's a good place to write. Many landmarks of our life together are here, like the theater where my brother directed and Dennis used to act, the bars where we used to drink, the settings for a lot of stories we've written. You can see the white concrete-block building where we first went to meetings after getting sober. You can see the church we belong to now. You can see Twentieth Street hill, which leads to Vulcan, the big statue who holds a torch that burns red if somebody's been killed in a car accident during the past twenty-four hours, green if nobody has. We almost rented a loft that faced east. We would have had a view of the viaduct that takes you to the neighborhood where we grew up. But we took this one, facing south, instead. It faces the cut through the mountain, the one that takes you directly to our present address. During the day, we can write in the loft. We can remember. We can make up things if we want. But in the end, we go home to children.

Marriage is like a rain forest. You have the canopy and the understory. The story of a marriage contains all that grows in the canopy, all that is visible from an aerial, or public, view. The understory of a marriage is the place where other things thrive. It is in the understory that we struggle, fight, and conceive. It's the place where we toss things, where compost is made, where anything can grow, including forgiveness.

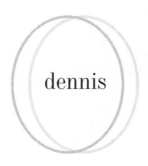

dennis

Two months after the woman with the letters showed up at our door, Vicki and I were in a sculpture garden in Phoenix, Arizona—a place so foreign, so distant from Birmingham, that we could have chosen it intentionally as a point of ulti-mate exile. While our daughters ran ahead to look at the other exhibits, we paused in front of a sculpture of a fully clothed woman lying on her side, as serene and silver as a fish. The woman's hands were folded on her chest; she appeared to be half-awake, but still dreaming. The piece was called *A Woman in Love*.

I turned to say how much I liked the sculpture, and when I did, I saw that Vicki's eyes had filled with tears.

I had an urge to embrace her, or hit her, I didn't know which. I couldn't stand to see her in pain, but this time the source of her pain was an affront. I didn't have a right to be mad, though. I had been seeing someone else, a woman I'll call Chance, almost precisely as long as Vicki had been seeing Kira's husband.

Chance was from our neck of the woods, the daughter of an east Birmingham steelworker. She was also a colleague of mine, a sculptor who taught night classes in the art department and fashioned miniature chairs out of materials like cobalt and titanium. She had always been an artist, but not always an academic. Like many women from our part of town, she had married young and spent a number of years as a dutiful wife and mother before coming back to the university to teach. She had a sharp, wise look about her, a tomboy grown up to be lean and wary; nobody's fool, but also, in ways, an innocent. That's what attracted me.

We had coffee together a few times that spring. We talked about our classes, our work, but I could tell that my attention was making her uncomfortable. When the quarter ended, I asked her to meet me again for coffee. At first she said yes, she was coming to that end of town anyway, but then she called back to cancel. Her son, she said, was with her.

Later, she left a message on my office answering machine. She was calling from the nearby interstate on her cellular phone to tell me there was a rainbow in the sky above the university. "I wonder if it's a sign," she said.

Less than ten minutes later, Chance lost control of her car. It hydroplaned across two lanes of traffic and then across the interstate's grassy median before plowing headlong into a car coming from the opposite direction. Chance escaped with cuts and abrasions. Her son, belted into a child's safety seat in the rear, was unscathed. But the sole occupant of the other car, a young woman on her way to lunch, had to be extricated from the wreckage with a tool called the "jaws of life" and flown by helicopter to a local hospital.

16

This is what Chance told me when I returned her phone message that afternoon. It was a startling beginning to a conversation that would last for hours, interrupted only by the arrival of Chance's neighbors and family, her minister, the police. Chance's husband was out of town, and her friends had gathered to give support. But somehow our phone conversation kept on, in fits and starts, all afternoon. For her, it must have been a kind of relief from trauma. For me, I see now, it was an antidote to loneliness—the peculiar loneliness of a family man.

The next day I left for Florida, but that night I called Chance from the road. The driver of the other car, she said, had died. We talked late into the night. We told each other our secrets, our stories, as though we were prison mates tapping on walls or survivors of some natural disaster. It was as though we were falling in love.

Maybe we were. Our conversation was still going on the next spring, when Vicki and the girls and I found ourselves in the sculpture garden of the museum in Phoenix. By then, Vicki knew about Chance and I knew about Kira's husband. For some months Vicki and I had been honest on the major points, but we had continued to deceive one another in countless other ways. There was no moral high ground for either of us to occupy. We seemed to be beyond redemption as we stared at the statue of a woman in love while our daughters begged to see the rest of the museum.

This was clearly not what we had in mind for the book. The hard times our marriage had gone through were supposed to be in the past. We'd already experienced the reckless, destructive episodes, the drinking and whoring around, and by now we were supposed to have recovered our senses. We'd sobered up, started a family, begun to make something of our lives. Chance and Kira's husband were not part of this scenario.

Our daughters, twelve and nine at the time, were exceptionally perceptive, but we were uncertain what they suspected or knew. Their faces that spring were as difficult to read as the surface of water at the bottom of the well they had helped me drill two days before we left for Phoenix.

Vicki and the girls had been tilling a patch of our side yard in order to plant a vegetable garden. I wanted to look for water as an experiment, so the girls could try out the equipment I'd bought for our upcoming trip to El Salvador. We probably wouldn't find water, I told them, but there was always a chance. And if we did find water, maybe we could use it to irrigate the garden.

The auger set was a two-piece model, designed to be operated by hand. It consisted of a shaft, a handle, and two kinds of auger heads, one shaped like an eggbeater with a single, sharp blade and the other shaped like a bucket with teeth. The augers could be attached to the handle and shaft by a series of extensions with bayonet couplings. The drilling itself was simple. We turned the auger clockwise, and it bit easily into the ground. Then we pulled it up, emptied the auger head, and reinserted it into the hole, adding extensions as we needed them.

Our first hole came up dry at less than eight feet, nothing but clay, thin layers of shale, and the hard clunk of apparent bedrock. Vicki took a rest from her tilling and left to do some grocery shopping, but Ashley insisted we try another spot at the end of the garden closest to the street. She was sure we would find water there, and she worked like a woman possessed.

At this site, we encountered the same clay and the same layers of shale, but we were able to go farther down, and at nine and a half feet we hit gray sand. There we had to stop. Neither of our auger heads would bring up the gray sand. It was too fine, we thought, until we plumbed the hole and discovered there was already a foot and a half of water at the bottom, water that lay on a shelf of solid rock. The gray sand had been an aquifer. We had indeed struck water in our own side yard, and the realization made us giddy. We were whooping and hollering by the time Vicki, her car filled with groceries, pulled up.

By then, it was almost dark. Low in the northwest sky, the Hale-Bopp comet had appeared, shedding its pale corona of light. The four of us gathered at the mouth of the hole. We dropped pieces of gravel down the hole and listened to the splash. We measured with a weighted tape, and listened again and again to the *plop* when the weight broke the surface of water. Each time, we looked at each other with mock surprise, as though we had discovered the water anew.

After I cased the well with two-inch PVC pipe, we got a flashlight from the kitchen and shone it down the length of the casing. It was genuinely dark by now, and we were huddled together on the ground. I wondered what the neighbors would think.

Laura saw the reflection on the water first, then Vicki, then me. Ashley looked last.

"I can see it now," she said, but in a flat and exacting tone that made me wonder if she really had.

"Did you really see it?" I asked when she stood up.

"Yes. I saw it," she said. And she looked at me hard before she turned off the flashlight and headed back toward the house. I was sure, in that moment, that she knew.

I don't think my own father was ever unfaithful to my mother, or she to him. But compared to what my daughters know about us, my parents' lives, before and after their marriage, constitute a kind of mystery. What I know for certain is that my father was a handsome man who liked to dance. We have photos of him in the white linen suit he wore to the Cloud Room behind Cascade Plunge on those Friday nights in the late twenties when all of Birmingham must have been dancing.

Mother does not appear in these photographs. Perhaps my father took other girls to the dances. Or perhaps he and his friends went stag. My sister Jeanie's theory is that Dad would have led a richer, fuller life if only he had married someone who liked to dance. But my father must have had his reasons for falling in love with Mother. Her own photos from the twenties are of a girl with long blond curls and a flawless, but troubling face. Her smile is frank. A childhood in the mining camps does not appear to have broken her spirit. It's true, though, that she did not like to dance. And perhaps that accounts for some of my own peculiarities. I was born to a man who liked to dance, and to a woman who didn't.

When I was still an infant, Dad would take Jeanie and her friend Mary Sue Stevens skating at a roller rink on the other side of town, near the steel mill where my father worked. Sometimes, Jeanie said, they ran into a woman there, someone from the mill. Jeanie remembers watching as my father and this woman circled the rink, thinking how beautifully they skated. Only in retrospect, she said, did it occur to her that there might have been a romantic connection.

But by the time she told me this story, our father was no longer alive. And I was forty-eight years old, with two young daughters who were not ready, I thought, to see the possibility of romance for me or their mother outside the love that had given them life.

For Vicki and me, romance and sex had been nearly two separate things. We had come of age during the sixties and early seventies. "It's your *thang*," the song went, ". . . do what you want to do," and the notion carried over painfully into our affair and marriage. We didn't have what used to be called an "open marriage." But we understood from the beginning that we would be powerfully attracted to other people. The only uncertainty was the degree of pleasure or pain we might cause one another as a result.

In short, we suffered through those years, and then we sobered up. Our girls came along, and we thought that their births would forever put an end to this particular kind of carelessness. How could we look at our daughters without acknowledging the irrevocable claim sex had on our emotions and faith?

.   .   .

In Phoenix, perhaps Ashley and Laura thought their mother's tears were a consequence of the difficult time she'd been having trying to care for her ailing parents. Or perhaps our daughters didn't notice the change in Vicki, not even when she insisted we go ahead with our Saturday plans to drive from Phoenix to the Grand Canyon, despite the storm that had left three feet of snow in Flagstaff. Vicki's relations with men notwithstanding, she has never been one to take off in unexpected directions. She always wants to know what to expect before she gets to a place, and if it's not what she hoped for, there's usually hell to pay. The day before, the road to the canyon had been closed. We didn't know the current conditions. But Vicki was up for hitting the road and going as far as we could. She shrugged when I reminded her we didn't have snow tires or chains.

"At least we'll see some snow," she said.

I also hoped we'd see Hale-Bopp above the Grand Canyon.

So we left for the canyon in short sleeves and without coats. It was deceptively sunny and dry outside Phoenix, a baked landscape we'd never seen before. I didn't much like it. I preferred cold empty spaces—the high flatlands of Wyoming and Montana, for instance, with sagebrush, tumbleweed, and sheer white mountains behind. But Vicki immediately took to the desert. It was like her life, she said, without a trace of irony. Only the creosote bushes along the interstate were in bloom, tiny yellow blossoms like those on the forsythia back home. But occasionally we would see cactus flowers, and Vicki began to take these as signs.

On the high plateaus near the turnoff to Sedona, we encountered the first frost, and by the time we approached Flag-staff, as though we had journeyed backward in time to December, the ground was covered in deep snow. Snow sat stacked on the branches of the ponderosa pines, and flakes hit the windshield in bursts. So far the road was still clear, but the wind had picked up. Drifting snow was blowing from the shoulders, and we were sure we'd have to end our journey in Flagstaff, at a Days Inn or Best Western across from a *faux*-Alpine mall. But at a highway intersection, a gas station attendant told us the road to the Grand Canyon was open. "You at least ought to be able to make it there," he said.

So we layered ourselves and kept on going, past frozen mountains, fields of untouched snow, forests in which elk foraged for buried growth. The girls were strangely subdued— no bickering from the back seat this time. It was as though they sensed that our lives were raw and open in a way they'd never been before, vulnerable to the slightest disturbance.

And what is there to say about the Grand Canyon? We came upon it just before sunset. The north rim was sheathed in a layer of light as fine as beaten gold. The river below was dark and sinuous, the walls a vivid ocher. The scale defied language. We were in the presence of God.

We did what we could. We found something to eat. We settled into our room. We were tourists who had made it to our destination. But I had forgotten that I wanted to see Hale-Bopp above the canyon until I walked to the gift shop that night to buy sweatshirts. And there was the comet in its customary place, the brightness of its tail intensified by the lack of competing artificial lights. I stood stunned by the singularity of the moment. Then I realized I was indeed seeing

Hale-Bopp above the Grand Canyon, but that it was too dark to see the canyon itself.

Certain law-enforcement agencies employ devices that are able to identify individual employees by the pattern of blood vessels in their eyes. You look into a peephole. An instrument makes its observation, draws an instant conclusion, and then opens the door or not. If the pattern of the vessels inside your eye does not match a pattern stored in the device's memory, you are locked out.

What happens when both the observed and the observer are human, eye meeting eye, each recording, searching its memory bank, drawing a conclusion, and then denying or yielding access? When was the last time Vicki and I truly had looked into each other's eyes, and what had we seen when we did? During the previous year, it seemed as though we had been looking through eyes that were clouded, milky, as though we were snakes about to shed our skins. In the process of sloughing off the old self, we were temporarily blinded. We couldn't see one another clearly, because if we could, then maybe the shedding would not, could not occur. If we saw clearly enough, maybe we would never want to meta-morphose, maybe we would realize that what we thought we were yearning for had been there all along.

Maybe the psyche draws its shades down before it makes a calculated leap, knowing that if it didn't, it would see to the bottom of the canyon and know how far it was risking a fall. And perhaps the tragedy of late middle age is the picture of us all standing, half blind at the edge of some abyss, unsure whether to leap before the light goes out entirely or to wait until our vision clears.

After Arizona, a call from Kira's husband sent Vicki into a tailspin. She told me at the kitchen table that she didn't want to live anymore. "Don't worry, I'm not going to kill myself," she said. "I just don't care whether I live or not. I even thought about it on the flight back from Phoenix, how it didn't matter if the plane went down. We were all together anyway, us and the girls."

Her doctor doubled her prescription for Prozac.

And I did an unspeakable thing. I told Chance that Vicki knew about her. The really unspeakable thing was that I had not told her from the beginning. Chance had suspected, of course. I think she even knew, had grown to know it the more I revealed about myself. But she rarely pressed me on the issue, and on those occasions when she did, I continued to lie. I was afraid the truth would kill her desire for me, and I didn't know how I could live without that.

Then came Arizona and its aftermath. In the middle of an ordinary conversation, I blurted out the truth. Chance and I had been talking about the book Vicki and I were writing. Chance reminded me that I had once told her I was scrupulously honest in my writing, if not my life. What did this mean in terms of the book?

I told her I would have to tell the truth in the book. There had never been any real question about that. Vicki and I might deceive each other in our marriage, might harbor resentments that we'd never speak, might shade and color our feelings in order to sustain each other's trust, but when it came to the written page, we were bound by a different code. We were writers first, husband and wife second, and as writers we could not, even in fiction, dissemble. The story itself was our only truth.

So I told Chance the truth, that Vicki had known about her for almost a year, since a night in late June, in upstate New York, on the night of my editor's wedding, when we lay in bed looking up at the ceiling. I'd told Vicki I thought there was someone else for her. She'd had the same feeling about me. We revealed it in a finger game like paper, scissors, rock. We took turns asking each other questions and responded simultaneously by holding up one finger or two, one for yes, two for no. Does he go to our church? Is she a neighbor of ours? Do you love him? Do you love her? The answers to the last two were ones. Then I told Vicki I knew who she was seeing. I told her his name. She was surprised. She couldn't guess the name of the woman I was seeing. When I told her, she paused and then nodded. It made sense, now that she thought about it. The name had come up more than once. She should have guessed.

I told Chance all this, about the night of the wedding, the finger game in bed. She already knew about the wedding itself, that my editor had asked me to read the chapter in Corinthians about love, and that the sermon had been a reflection on the line from the Auden poem "Tell Me the Truth about Love."

That was a Friday. On Monday I called Chance and asked her how she felt. "How do I feel?" she said. "How do I feel? I feel like a chapter in a fucking book."

This, Vicki says, is where the book begins.

in the quick

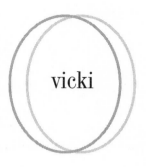

vicki

I was a shy, smart, big kid. I was afraid of the dark, and of people who wore glasses. It must have been hard on Mother, having to apologize to innocent bystanders in their bifocals when I'd let loose a bloodcurdling scream. I think it was nearsightedness, which I'd grow to have myself, that scared me—the Coke bottle–lens effect that made people's eyes loom larger than life. Eyes, in general, scared me. My Aunt Weeby had a wandering eye, and I hid from her. There was a man at church, in the choir, whose eyeballs bulged. They grew larger and brighter, word by word—"Holy, HOLY, HOLY!"—as I shrank down from the pew to the floor thinking, I'm going to die.

I thought a lot about dying. Sometimes I'd think about it on summer nights when we played outside. If you were *it*—and I generally was *it*, unless I faked an asthma attack to get out of being *it*—you'd sit on top of Eighth Avenue Hill on a car with a flashlight. If you weren't *it*, you'd crawl belly-to-earth like a snake in the grass, trying to stay away from the orb of light. There we all were under the stars, happier than we'd ever be in life, but it was all screwed up for me because of gravity. I'd think, We might be upside down at this very moment, panic, grab a nandina bush, get caught in the flashlight, and have to be *it* again. And as if the laws of nature weren't enough, there we were in Birmingham feeling lowdown as hell, because every time we went to Florida on vacation there were Yankees on the beach saying, "Birmingham, oh Jesus, what a place to be from," in that nasal superiority that spun me into acute anxiety. I'd lie on the bed and ask Mother to feel my heart pounding.

I started wondering if I had Problems. I bit my nails to the quick, the word Mother used. She'd say, "You've bitten down to the quick." It wasn't an accusation, it was an observation. We might stare at my fingers. We might be in the car, at a railroad crossing, as we surveyed the quick—the raw flesh, the living vital core of a thing. That's what I was after.

Before long, I was having full-blown panic attacks. I didn't know what they were, and neither did anybody around me, in that pre-therapy era. Depersonalization was simply the "dreamy" feeling. Claustrophobia was the "this place is on fire and nobody knows it but me" feeling. I associated it all with Cuba, because I'd never gotten over the Crisis, when the Whittens up on Ninth Avenue bulldozed their front yard to build a bomb shelter and June, my best friend's mother, stocked her basement with canned figs. In the basement at the Williamses', where my Girl Scout troop met, water jugs stood ready for nuclear attack. Yellow warning signs shaped like triangles, fallout shelters, raids, drills—these were bad things for a girl who'd just gotten over being scared of people's eyes. And since I had asthma, I carried a fear of drowning—not in a swimming pool, but in my own bed in my own urine. I wet the bed way past the time when most kids stop. We didn't have clinical jargon for that either, but I made sure to become a therapist later in life in order to learn terms like *enuresis* and *encopresis* and *neurosis*. I never cozied to the practice of psychotherapy, but I did have a passion for the *Diagnostic and Statistical Manual*. I liked making sense of things.

But that's jumping ahead.

It's Christmas Eve, 1964. My family is gathered at Aunt Weeby's house for dinner. This is my father's side of the family. One wing is composed of actors. The other wing is made up of peculiar introverts who are preoccupied with germs. The introverts eat at a separate table so they won't get the actors' germs. They even bring their own food. My family—Daddy, Mother, my big brother, Randy, and me—eat with the actors. This table is boisterous and I wonder if I don't maybe belong at the other table, where people toy with their food and keep quiet. But after dinner is over and we have eaten lane cake and ambrosia, the two tables unite in a candlelit Christmas Eve ritual. My Uncle Claude sets off firecrackers in the back yard while Aunt Weeby arranges the chairs (which she's covered with plastic) for the big performance. First they make me play my piano recital piece. Afterward, Daddy and Randy give interpretive readings of Christ's birth from Luke 2. They read the same passage, but they say it differently, inflecting different words. Aunt Weeby cries. Then my cousin Julie, who is a gymnast, does cartwheels and backflips, careful not to tump over the Christmas tree. "She's going to be a cheerleader at the University of Alabama," they all correctly predict. For the grand finale my Uncle Buddum pulls out his guitar and sings Frank Sinatra's "My Way." What all this has to do with the birth of Christ is beyond me, but it is against this family setting that I feel real panic crawl up my spine.

I don't say a word. I just get up and go to Aunt Weeby's front porch. Aunt Weeby has a passion for Christmas lights. Miles of them. The door, the windows, the awning, the wrought-iron furniture, the shrubs are all flashing red, green, yellow, and blue when I go to the porch, my heart beating madly. In the midst of this being-on-fire sensation, I start to disappear. I sit in a swing, and bit by bit I recede from my environment. When Mother comes out to check on me, I tell her, "I'm dreaming."

"No, you're not," she says. "You're at Aunt Weeby's."

She sits with me on the porch while my Uncle Buddum's baritone drifts back to us:

> *The record shows, I took the blows*
> *And did it my way.*

Mother doesn't say a word. I like having her nearby, but my plight is inexplicable.

"I'm going to faint," I tell her.

"Okay," she replies.

I put my head between my legs, because I've heard of people doing this. Mother says, "Aunt Weeby's going to hand out presents now." We go back inside. I try to act normal, even though I'm depersonalized. Aunt Weeby gives me a hair dryer for Christmas, the kind with the plastic cap that zips into a round suitcase.

If I'd known how, I might have been able to step back, light up, and take a long, scorching draw of myself, as I later learned to do by writing. But I didn't know how in those days. Instead, I spent the rest of Christmas Eve wondering how Aunt Weeby's yard would look after the Russians dropped the atomic bomb. By the time we left her place, I'd collected myself. We drove past the landmarks on Warrior Road—the site of my drunk granddaddy's gas station; U.S. Steel, where my sober granddaddy worked in the tin mill before his heart attack; through downtown Birmingham, where my parents had spent their wartime honeymoon at the Tutwiler Hotel; over the viaduct with the pig-iron furnaces below; and on into our neighborhood of Crestwood, which was a subdivision directly off the Atlanta Highway. We never went to Atlanta, but maybe living near the highway gave foundrymen like my dad, who'd grown up dirt-poor, a sense of possibility.

We crossed the railroad tracks. We bypassed the midsection, where we lived, and went on up to the nice section— Bull Connor's neighborhood—where there were elaborate manger scenes in the yards and as many Christmas lights as Aunt Weeby's. We checked to see who'd won first, second, and third prizes for decoration. Then we went home to our small, ranch-style brick. I lay in bed. I could hear our neighbor's rock-polishing machine churning in the carport. I got up and looked out my window at the Vests' house. The mother, Hazel, was from England, a war bride who had met

Floyd at a USO club and who fixed martinis at dusk but stashed them in the oven if neighbors dropped by, which caused a lot of shattered glass. The father, Floyd, had a closetful of *Playboys* that I looked at whenever I possibly could. Their son, Buddy, was my slave. I made him pee in the shrubs.

But as I sat by my window on Christmas Eve, my heart no longer racing with panic, I wasn't thinking of Hazel or Floyd or Buddy. I was thinking of the Vests' daughter, Glenda. I was waiting for her to come home with her boyfriend, Jimmy Dorriety, who was tall and dark and chiseled-looking. Glenda was going to bring him to my window. She was going to toss a rock up to let me know it was time. Jimmy was going to turn her to him in the moonlight, put a hand under her chin, and kiss her.

I heard the car coming. They parked on the street. I saw them look directly at my window as if it held a charm. They walked toward my driveway, and my heart started going, not with panic, but with anticipation. Jimmy put his arms around her waist. I loved the sight of her hungry hands.

There they were, in a single night, the three things that were going to collide in me for most all of my life: panic, lust, and the birth of Christ.

I didn't have any more panic attacks until the following September, when my grandmother took my best friend, Carol Callaway, and me to the Cerebral Palsy Telethon, which was held every year at the Boutwell Auditorium in downtown Birmingham. My grandmother Ma Marsh was a strong woman. She'd married a drunk, which meant she'd worked hard all her life. Ma Marsh liked taking us places. She'd volunteered to take Carol and me to the telethon. The event always drew movie stars who helped raise money for this worthy cause. That year, Edd "Kookie" Byrnes from the television show 77 *Sunset Strip* had come. It was very special having him in Birmingham. I was sitting on a ledge with my autograph book in hand. Kookie came to the stage and pulled a comb from his back pocket. The minute he did this, I turned to my grandmother.

"I'm going to faint," I told her.

She smiled like it was because I was seeing Edd Byrnes in the flesh.

"No, really," I said, my heart revving up just as it had on Christmas Eve at Aunt Weeby's. "I'm going to die," I told her.

Carol said, "Let's go up there. Let's get his autograph." We'd been looking forward to this moment. But I held back. In the end, we missed the opportunity and only got the autograph of Country Boy Eddie, a local TV personality who was on Channel 6 at daybreak. By the time we left the auditorium, my heart rate was normal and the depersonalization had subsided, but I remember how eerie the night felt, how the sky was gray-blue like X-rays, and how worried I was because Birmingham would be a likely candidate for the bomb, since we manufactured pig iron. Everywhere you went in Birmingham you saw the big blast furnaces with streams of molten steel.

"They'll get us right after they get Washington, D.C.," somebody's parents said.

We left the auditorium and drove back home over the viaduct. I didn't look down, but I knew the liquid metal was being poured. I knew they were tapping the furnaces. I knew the bombs were being readied for an attack on Birmingham. I looked at Carol. Fair-skinned and fresh, she'd lost her front teeth in a violent accident during PE. It made me love her. "Spend the night with me," she said. When we got home, Mother packed my suitcase and we walked down the hill to Carol's house. A mimosa tree grew in Carol's yard, and if you climbed high enough, you could see the power yard that dropped to a ravine where railroad tracks separated us from blacks.

Carol's bedroom smelled like eggs. Carol's mother, June, made her eat scrambled eggs, which she hated, so every morning when her mother turned to wash the dishes, Carol slid the eggs into her napkin and later deposited them in her desk drawer. At the end of the week she fed the eggs to her dog, Frisky.

We must have talked about the usual things in bed—the neighborhood, when to dispose of the bad eggs, boys. We may have practiced kissing, which we did frequently. Carol always let me choose whether to be the boy or the girl, depending on what mood I was in. But all I remember is that sometime in the middle of the night I fell off the bed. My body hit the hardwood floor with a thud so strong it woke Carol's mother. She flew into Carol's room shouting, "It's hit! The bomb!"

"Vicki fell off the bed," Carol mumbled to her, groggy from sleep.

June wiped her forehead. I felt bad. June had migraines,

and once she'd put a sewing-machine needle through her finger and fainted.

"I was in the middle of a nightmare," she told me, sitting on the edge of Carol's bed. "World War III had started, and I'd just stuffed Carol down the drainpipe in the back yard when you hit the floor."

This scared the shit out of me. I knew the drain she was talking about. Water often collected in it. I generalized this, as I was prone to do, into a fear of all drains. Anything resembling a well began to frighten me. Empty swimming pools with exposed drains still bother me. The first time I ever went to see a shrink at age twenty-seven I described myself as a girl in the depths of a dark well. I told him—immediately, after five minutes—that he was the man at the top, and I wanted him to save me. He wrote Adjustment Disorder with Depressed Mood on the insurance form and gave me antidepressants, which I didn't take. But that's way on into the story.

Fortunately, the other guy blinked, and Cuba dismantled the missiles. I never again fell off Carol's bed during the night, and her mother quit having nightmares about war. Neighbors took the canned figs and water jugs from their basements, and I guess the Whittens up on Ninth Avenue resigned themselves to the fact that they'd always have a bomb shelter under their lawn.

Water was all over my neighborhood. If I hadn't been so preoccupied with bombs, I might have taken note of how safe and lush the place really was. Water was in plastic swimming pools, in buckets, flowing from garden hoses. We had one of those green strips that makes the water shoot up in threads. I'd stand over it, letting the water go up my legs, loving it, craving it. Drinking it. Thirst, summer thirst, where you can't get enough, can't possibly make the longing in your throat go away, was, for me, the forerunner of lust.

During the summer we went to Cascade Plunge almost every day. Cascade Plunge was the community pool, where a radio station broadcast music from a glass booth and teen-agers danced on the deck and Little Peggy March belted, "I will follow him, follow him wherever he may go." I liked that song. I liked to think of love as something unmanageable and desperate. The next October, when I was twelve, I tasted it for the first time. I was lying in the grass in my front yard. I'd been playing football with the boys. We played slow-motion tackle, where you ran softly and leaped like a dancer. It was a kind of crude ballet with a trace of violence. I had the ball. A boy named Pat Hall tackled me. He was Catholic, with blue eyes. I'd been tackled before, but something was different this time. Instead of getting up, he straddled me. My hands were over my head, palms up. I struggled, but he pressed my hands hard, harder. I got still. He'd nailed me. I knew we weren't playing football anymore, even before Mother called me inside and told me I was too old to play football with boys.

Pat is as fresh in my mind as what I ate for lunch today. He was the birth of desire, but I felt it as thirst. I still do. Hunger is multifaceted. You can be hungry for carbohydrates or beef or chocolate pie. But thirst is singular.

I don't remember what became of Pat. I think he must have gone to a parochial school or moved away. But he'd quickened something in me, and I knew I didn't have to watch Glenda Vest and Jimmy Dorriety kiss in my driveway now. I didn't have to practice with Carol. I could have the real thing, and by 1967 I was lost in love. I liked all its stages, and I wanted to be in every stage, at every moment. So I had a boyfriend, a side boyfriend, a past boyfriend, and a future boyfriend. The past boyfriend was the most interesting, because I liked to hurt. Whenever I got jilted, my brother would come into my bedroom and tell me things like "Time is your friend." Sometimes he'd bring home one of his buddies. One of them was Dennis Covington.

Dennis was from East Lake, a neighborhood close to ours. East Lake had fights and junkyard thefts and smoke bombs that went awry, burning up garages. Dennis was a kind of intellectual James Dean. He was the first to swing from a rope in the high school auditorium's balcony to the stage below, the first to damn segregation, to read the Russian writers, to take LSD, to write a story, get a motorcycle, ride it naked, leave home.

He was four years older than me, a big gap. But we saw the same sights, heard the same sounds, knew the same people. We sat in the same high school auditorium and stared at the same mural that depicted cultural demise under the hand of the industrial revolution—a boy and a girl coming into the world through a blue globe, a woman chained to a gear where a muscled man is saving or killing her, take your pick; a Nazi boy holding a sword to a nymphet; deformed faces, foundries, mines, and train yards; telephone poles bending in the wind. This is what we saw, day after day. In time, foundries and deformity would be things we'd write about. But we didn't know it then. We didn't have a clue.

I kept having panic attacks. My driver's license was a problem. I wanted to drive. I did drive. But the steering wheel of an automobile is a bad place for a phobic. I didn't like streets with no guardrails, streets that dropped to ravines. Birmingham is a series of hills and valleys, and this posed problems. The worst spot was on Highway 78, the Atlanta Highway, on the way back from Eastwood Mall. Eastwood Mall was the only mall in Birmingham, and everything happened there. But on the way home, the road snaked a bit, dropping off to a driving range called Sam Byrd's, where my dad hit yellow golf balls into a dark sky on summer nights. Now I had a fear of purposely driving my daddy's Chevrolet over the edge. I'd sail, mentally, right over the pine trees to the clubhouse below, crashing into the wire buckets of yellow golf balls. In church I was afraid of losing control and screaming "Goddamn!" to no one in particular.

I'd later learn that the fear of yelling obscenities in inappropriate settings is a symptom of obsessive-compulsive personality disorder, but I wasn't a therapist when I was sixteen. I was Vicki Marsh, and I'm certain I appeared to be just fine, which was what you said when people asked how you were doing. Mother made my clothes, and they were simple and colorful and fit me well. I didn't have an eating disorder. I made A's. I was a member of the National Honor Society. I played Bach two-part inventions with precision. My parents were exceedingly proud of my accomplishments. I went parking every Friday night and kept myself, technically, a virgin. I didn't smoke.

My nails were still a mess, though, and Mother was noting, "You're in the quick," as she dropped me off at Dot Smith's, where I took piano. Beethoven, Rachmaninoff, Chopin,

Liszt, Bach, all had a way of coming through my hands, but there was always longing with the satisfaction, and I interpreted longing as emptiness and emptiness as thirst and thirst as love. I was playing some difficult pieces by now— Rachmaninoff's Prelude in C# Minor, Chopin's Military Polonaise, Debussy's Arabesque No. 1. I didn't know I was accomplished. It felt more like swimming. Dot let me interpret the music. Plus, Dot was a nail-biter. "If you didn't bite them, I'd have to cut them anyhow," she told me.

I liked her for this. I liked her, period. She let me play it like I wanted to. Mother and Daddy were the same way, in regard to me. I was free to make a mess of my life, and I was on the brink of doing it.

I was a member of a sorority. At Christmas we'd take turns being Santa's helpers at Eastwood Mall, where the jolly man had flown in the day after Thanksgiving in a helicopter. We, the Phi Betas, dressed up in skimpy red velvet outfits that left plenty of leg showing for Santa. We helped kids make their way to Santa's big lap while our boyfriends stood nearby. My boyfriend was named Jerry. My friend Lisa dated a Jerry, too. Her Jerry was bad news. He had a violent nature that generally turned itself inward. He would, in time, stick a gun down his throat and videotape his own suicide. He was from East Lake. My other friend, Jane, was dating David Granger, who later became a star running back at Tennessee. Granger didn't live with his parents, I don't remember why. He had an apartment. This was not ordinary. In December 1969, when I was seventeen and we'd been Santa's helpers that night, Jane and Lisa and I went to Granger's apartment with both Jerrys.

It was cold, and Granger was tossing his dirty dishes down to the parking lot because he didn't want to wash them. I didn't yet understand this kind of logic. I didn't yet know liquor. My dad didn't drink it, because his dad was alcoholic. Mother didn't drink it, because Daddy didn't drink it. I didn't want to drink it, because my boyfriend, Jerry, drank it, and when he did he always looked up his former girlfriend, a redhead named Janet. This night, Jerry and I sat at the kitchen table of Granger's apartment, watching his plates sail like flying saucers into the winter sky. He kept tossing them, occasionally turning to grin at us.

Jerry had dark eyes. On the table was a bottle of Jack Daniel's. "It's bourbon," he was telling me. He wanted me to have a drink. I was debating it. I asked him how to drink it. He said he'd mix it with Coke or ginger ale if I'd like, but I might just want it over ice, strong. I don't know how he knew this about me. I was quiet and spacey, not daring. He studied me like a lawyer or a broker, like somebody wanting to advise correctly. "Pour it," I told him. He did, over ice. I drank it. I knew it for what it was: my life for the following thirteen years.

To this day—and I haven't had a drop since I quit at thirty—to this day, I crave the power of alcohol. The way it burns. The way it burns away fear. That night, all of David Granger's dishes were in the parking lot, broken. Jerry and I sat at the table. It was winter 1969.

And I drank.

Liquor was better than love. It was very reliable and didn't break up with you. Jerry left my life and joined the Navy. I got a smart boyfriend named Bill. I went to the University of Alabama. I liked pot. I hated college. I didn't fit. I didn't like the quadrangle. I didn't like being rejected by rich girls who knew I'd gone to a blue-collar high school. I didn't like riding my bicycle to see a guy named Adrian, who would give me a joint. I didn't like trying to figure out that song, "You put the lime in the coconut and drink it all up." I didn't like making a D in basic algebra. I didn't like it that my boyfriend, Bill, left me for a redheaded actress. I didn't like redheads. I didn't like opening my post-office box at the student union building, dying of thirst for my mother's letter. I didn't think it was natural, missing her so much.

I moved back home. For a year I went to the university's Birmingham campus and studied Spanish. I worked at a bookstore. I didn't drink. I didn't have a boyfriend. It felt significant. It seemed such a serious moment, being out of love. My parents bought me an airline ticket to go see Uncle Buddum. This was the thing to do if you were in the midst of a good or a bad crisis—you went to see Buddum. His real name was Jim, and he was a preacher. He'd left the Baptist Church in the mid-sixties, when a deacon punched him in the face for saying that black people were welcome at their church. He now had a sailboat and an interfaith church on Longboat Key in central Florida.

On the flight down I sat next to a man I remember vividly. He had brown eyes, and he told me he was thirty-five. While we ate our chicken Kiev, peas, and carrots, I told him my boyfriend had left me for a redheaded actress. I didn't tell him she had big breasts. I didn't tell him I was certain the plane was going to crash and that he was going to have to help me with the yellow oxygen mask. I didn't tell him I'd never flown alone or that I was scared of heights and depths. He wasn't wearing glasses, and his eyes were a normal size. That helped. I told him I was going to see my uncle, who had a guitar, a sailboat, and a way with words. After a while, he looked right at me and said, "You've got a lot of joy and pain ahead of you." When we got to the Tampa airport, I watched him disappear in the terminal. Since I'd never traveled, I wasn't used to brief interactions that seem mystical at the moment, and so I had a fleeting desire to run after him.

Instead, I went to the gift shop and bought myself a poster. On it was a midnight sky with a Camus quote: "In the midst of winter I finally learned that there was, in me, an invincible summer." My Uncle Buddum picked me up at the Tampa airport and we drove to Bradenton. I told Buddum that my boyfriend had left me, I'd moved back home, and I hadn't smoked any pot for several months. He took me to his friend Erston's place, and Erston put headphones on me and played a Vikki Carr album—the one with the song "Let it please be him, oh dear God, it must be him, or I shall die." I thought about the man on the plane, and what if I'd run after him and he'd turned and told me the exact nature of the joy and pain he saw in my future.

I was at a critical juncture, a fork in the road. For no matter how much I loved the poster with the Camus quote—and I hung it on every apartment wall I had for the next several years—no matter how I liked to believe it, I had *not* yet learned that there was, in me, an invincible summer. I didn't know what summer meant. It's not brutal sun or guts or a hard core. It's longing. In the Psalmist's words, it's "the hart panting after the brook."

That's the invincible thing I had in me.

When I got back to Birmingham, I started working with neighborhood kids near the inner-city church in which I had grown up. I thought of becoming a missionary. I came so close to choosing a purposeful life then, so close to taking a road other than the one I took. But my friend Lisa called one day asking if I wanted to go back to the Tuscaloosa campus and live with her in an apartment. I liked the word *apartment.* So I moved back. I got a new boyfriend named Daniel, who was working on a Ph.D. in political science. We smoked hash and listened to "Bolero" on bar stools under a blue light in his apartment. I studied sociology and psychology. I knew I still had Problems. I'd have panic attacks if the pot wasn't right, and I was very thirsty for Jack Daniel's most nights. I was *in the quick.* I started graduate school in social work, Daniel turned mean-when-drunk, and in the spring of 1975 I moved back to Birmingham to do a field placement at a rehab center where people with spinal-cord injuries were coming to terms with the fact that they would never use their legs. I lived alone in a high-rise that scared me because I was afraid of heights. I was afraid I'd jump.

I finished graduate school and got a job at a mental health center. I had a mixed caseload—depressed women, hyperactive kids, a child molester, and lots of schizophrenics who'd get a Prolixin injection every three weeks or a refill of Thorazine. A court order had recently emptied most of Alabama's state mental hospitals into halfway houses, so we were real busy. I liked the diagnosis Schizophrenia, Chronic Undifferentiated Type (CUT). I had a client named Margaret, who was a CUT. She believed that Jimmy Carter had been born in a stable to an elephant. Her delusions were crawling with incest, monkeys, Democrats, and, as she put it, "piles of cow dookey." I looked forward to seeing her. I think she put things in perspective for me, once and for all. For no matter how many panic attacks I had or how *in the quick* I might be, I did not believe that Jimmy Carter had been born to an elephant. I might have Problems, but next to Margaret I was the picture of health.

Randy, my brother, was married by now and directing plays at Birmingham Festival Theatre. Every Fourth of July, he'd have a big party. He lived above a golf course that gave a partial view of the city. On the night of July 4, 1975, there were a lot of water pipes and cat hair at his party. Nobody was eating hors d'oeuvres.

I know the details of what happened that night. What I can't remember is who I was, at twenty-two. All I know is, I was a social worker fascinated by mental disorder. I kept a tidy apartment. I drank Smirnoff. That night, I wove in and out of Randy's friends, who were the fabric of my life. I went to the kitchen, mixed a drink, and when I turned back to the living room, which was a tiny space with a hardwood floor, I ran into Dennis Covington.

"I have something to give you," I told him.

I pulled him into a back room, closed the door, and kissed him. It was as if he were a business associate and I'd taken him aside to hand him an urgent message. In actuality, I didn't know where he'd been all those years, that he'd been to Virginia and in the Army and to Iowa. I didn't know he was married to Susan. I didn't know he'd returned to Birmingham to teach at a black college on the west side of the city. All I knew was that I'd just kissed him for no reason and that I was staring down at his high-top sneakers. I let my eyes travel up his lean body, past his ivory shirt, to his lips.

I think I said, "I'm sorry."

I didn't know why—why I'd done this, why I was sorry, why we were standing there, hand in hand, surveying the situation.

We knew we were connected. We remembered. We remembered his being in and out of our house all those years. We knew each other for who we were. It wasn't going to be pretty or easy or necessarily fun. It was going to be messy. There was going to be tragedy, and we were going to manufacture every nut and bolt of it. We were going to drink vats of liquor. We were going to cry and lie and almost die, suffer, hurt each other in unspeakable ways. But we were also going to dig—manholes and foxholes and trenches—and I was not going to fall into a water well.

That night we simply turned and went back to the party. We talked afterward, of nothing in particular. I gave him my address, and a few days later he knocked on my door. A film crew was in Birmingham, shooting the movie *Stay Hungry*. They'd brought in some nice stuff—Acapulco gold. Dennis rolled a skinny joint in canary-yellow paper. We got high, and he told me it was Bastille Day. I took this as a sign. I was into signs. He started coming over to my apartment to do his and Susan's laundry in the basement of the building. I liked watching the way he folded Susan's things. But marriage was a mystery to me.

My brother was directing *Trouble in Tahiti,* a Leonard Bernstein opera about a troubled American marriage. On opening night I sat a few rows back from Dennis and Susan, at an angle where I had a good view of the two of them. There is a haunting song in the play. "There is a garden," a line goes. It's about trying to find your way back to a place you knew, a good place you're sure existed once, although you can't remember the place itself anymore. I watched Dennis and Susan listen to the song, and I knew that marriage was sad.

But I wanted it.

I wanted it with him.

A year later, Dennis got a job offer from the College of Wooster in Ohio. He left in a U-Haul, toting his motorcycle, trumpet, and sofa bed. Susan didn't go. They got a divorce, and I moved to Ohio the next year.

After living together four months, we flew back to Birmingham to get married—on Christmas Eve, 1977, in my parents' living room, where we promised each other nothing. But I did buy myself a wedding ring at Golbro's for $14. I still wear it. It is a symbol of simplicity, of grace, of the things we couldn't promise.

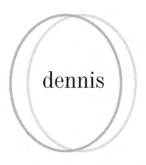

dennis

I grew up on Eightieth Street in a neighborhood called East Lake, an innocuous stretch of frame bungalows occupied mainly by the families of Birmingham grocers. Some of the fathers were also plumbers and carpenters and service-station owners. My own father worked in the office building at Tennessee Coal and Iron.

"I hope you never take up cigarettes," he said to me when I was eight and he was forty-four—too old, I thought, to be the father of anyone my age.

It was his day off, a Saturday, and he had been working at the kitchen table on the Sunday-school lesson he would be teaching the next morning to the Wesley Fellowship Class. The lesson was titled "How Great *Art* Thou?"—after the song popularized by George Beverly Shea—and it contained statistics from *Reader's Digest* about the size and complexity of the universe.

He tapped a Lucky Strike from its pack and struck a match with his thumbnail, inhaling the smoke as though he were gauging the depth of a mystery.

When my father exhaled, he did so in three distinct steps, first from his mouth in a narrow sideways stream and then out his nose, while he rolled the ash against the rim of the jelly lid he used in lieu of a proper ashtray. He always ended with a fine, voluminous cloud of smoke blown straight up toward the kitchen ceiling. The overall effect was impressive.

"You see what cigarettes have done to me," he said. And I did, although not in the way he meant.

At eight, I had never questioned the existence of God. He was apparent down the street, in the willows along the creek where the queen snakes sunned and in the shallows where the heron fished. My father, one of twelve children in another, grimier neighborhood, had walked alone to church, a boy compelled by wonder to seek out the maker of the world. I identified with him. And even when my skepticism would later prove too much to bear, I never questioned the sincerity of my father's faith. If there was a God, He would be like him.

That night, I pretended to fall asleep in the den so that my father would carry me up the stairs to my and my brother Gary's bedroom. Gary was twenty and due to go into the Army in September.

"He's an armful," Gary said.

"Like you, when you were his age," my father replied. He laid me on the bed and tucked in the covers. Then he opened the windows a crack.

"Good night, son," he said.

After my father left, Gary turned out the light. A moment later Mother appeared in the doorway. The yellow light from the hall fell on the oval throw rug, illuminating Gary's hunting boots and my genuine-leather moccasins and socks.

Mother's hands moved lightly over the spread. She kissed me on the cheek.

This was the summer after my sister, Jeanie, turned sixteen. One afternoon, while my mother gave Jeanie a Toni perm in the kitchen, I lay on the living-room rug, playing records on Jeanie's 45. My favorite records were by the Platters, Frankie Laine, and Johnny Mathis. I saved Johnny Mathis for last. "Wonderful, Wonderful" took me out of myself. I imagined I was on a cliff above the sea, the wind billowing, sunlight dancing all around, and Johnny Mathis's voice came to me as clear as the light, as urgent as the waves below.

It was more than the song that moved me, though. It was the secret I nursed in my heart. For I believed that Jeanie's boyfriend, a wiry East Lake boy named Don Moore, was actually Johnny Mathis. I had never heard Don sing in person, but I knew he was a soloist with the Warblers, the high school glee club. Jeanie was their accompanist. It did not matter to me that Johnny Mathis was a famous black entertainer and Don Moore was a diminutive white boy with a crew cut and a 1954 Ford. To me, they were one and the same. When I listened to Johnny Mathis on Jeanie's 45 player, it was Don Moore's voice I heard. It was his voice, clear and tender, that took me out of myself. I thought about asking him for his autograph, but I was afraid, and I knew that even if I did summon enough courage to ask, Don Moore would never sing "Wonderful, Wonderful" for me.

I never told anyone about this, or about the longing I had for the black girl who came to our front door selling peaches. She was always barefoot, and she carried four baskets of peaches by their wire handles, two in each hand. Her legs were as thin as pipe cleaners beneath her unsashed pinafore.

Her grandfather waited in the mule-drawn wagon by the curb. I used to imagine myself taking the girl's hand and leading her into the dark house. My parents would be away. I was going to save the black girl through some unspecified gesture of self-sacrifice, but I could never figure out what I would be saving her from.

This is what I knew about love when I was a child. And I think I began to leave my childhood when I realized that real life and make-believe were two separate things. My parents' marriage was much more complicated than I could have understood; my brother Gary would come back from the Army changed; Don Moore, my sister's boyfriend, wasn't Johnny Mathis after all; and the black girl who sold peaches door-to-door would never, ever come into our house, particularly if my parents were away.

In the summer of 1964, my friend Glenn Gaskins and I took a Greyhound bus to Atlanta, Georgia. Glenn was the first person in my school to own a transistor radio. "A Walk in the Black Forest" was the popular song.

In Atlanta, we walked to a store near a suburban park, where we bought two quart bottles of Country Club malt liquor. As we made our way back across the park, a group of older teenagers surrounded us.

"What have you got in the bag?" one of them asked.

"Bread," I said.

"So you're taking some bread home to your mother," he said. "I bet she's going to make shit sandwiches for you."

I nodded in agreement, and the other boys jeered. But when they let us pass, Glenn and I found a ravine under a highway overpass. There we turned the bottles up. It was the best I'd ever felt. We walked back across the park and into a drugstore. I turned over a cosmetics table. Glenn threw up later. I didn't get sick. I hoped I never would. I didn't know I already was.

When I drank after that, I always drank to get drunk—at the beach when I was sixteen, and in parked cars on neighborhood streets in the middle of the afternoon. I played trumpet in our high school band and in a rock-and-roll band called The Majestics. Our gigs were mostly dental or medical fraternity parties at the local university. We played songs like "Gloria" and "I Fought the Law (and the Law Won)" and "They Call Me Mister Pitiful," and I always stepped to the front for our instrumental, Herb Alpert's "The Lonely Bull." None of the other band members drank. But sometimes I was so drunk I couldn't get my lips to form an embouchure for "The Lonely Bull." It crossed my mind that alcohol could become a problem for me. God, whether He existed or not, was the least of my concerns.

I first saw Vicki in the summer of 1966, when I was seventeen and she was thirteen. I was standing in the living room of her family's house in Crestwood. I'd come home from school with her brother, Randy, a tough guy with a fragile heart, and I saw Vicki walk down the hall past the doorway to the living room. Her honey-blond hair was pulled back in a ponytail. She wore khaki-colored culottes. But it was her face that drew me. She had a perfect profile, and when she turned her head momentarily as she passed, I saw her wide green eyes and the lips that were set in a suggestion of the pout her brother Randy sometimes wore. Then Vicki smiled, and her smile took my breath. She was beautiful, and I remember thinking, It's too bad she's only thirteen.

I went out of state to college that fall, to the University of Virginia. I had a girlfriend there named Claire Miller. She was from west Texas, by way of Arlington, Virginia, and she and I had more fun than I'd ever thought possible. She was the only girl I'd known who was tall enough to look me in the eye while we danced. She gripped the lapels of my wool blazer and whispered, "What's mine is mine, what's yours is mine." We drank mostly rum drinks, daiquiris especially, and the smell of daiquiris in an airplane or restaurant to this day arouses in me the tragedy of love.

I loved Claire desperately and miserably, and when she wound up pregnant in the winter of my junior year, I asked her to marry me. She thanked me, but said she wanted to have an abortion instead, so I called Randy in Birmingham. Randy's girlfriend was a nurse and knew of an abortionist who operated out of a motel in Midfield, on the four-lane west of Birmingham called the Bessemer Super Highway. The cost would be $250, plus airfare and expenses for Claire and me. I borrowed some money from a college friend and from my older brother, Scotty, not telling either of them why, and asked Randy's girlfriend to make the appointment.

The technique was crude, but generally effective. The abortionist catheterized Claire's uterus, artificially dilating the cervix, and then packed her vagina with gauze. The abortion itself would occur several days later, as a consequence of the dilated cervix. But the first attempt didn't work. So a couple of weeks later Claire and I flew back to Birmingham, where we stayed again with Randy and his girlfriend, and Randy drove Claire to Midfield for a second try. Three days after we returned to Virginia, in the bathroom of her dormitory at Sweet Briar, Claire aborted the baby, flushed it down the toilet, and called to tell me how shocked she had been when she saw that it actually had hands and feet.

Claire eventually left me for an MBA. I saw our breakup as the single great tragedy of my life. I told my father about the abortion. He was understanding almost to a fault. I burned Claire's love letters. I thought about killing myself. Instead, I grew sideburns and became a campus radical. I also went to Randy's psychiatrist, who diagnosed situational depression and wrote a letter to my draft board advising them to defer me, an argument they bought—for a little while, anyway.

My dad let me take his Volkswagen Beetle back to Charlottesville after Christmas break. Outside Farmville, Virginia, I ran the VW off the road and into a cornfield. The investigating state trooper advised me to throw away anything I might not want him to find when he searched the car. I tossed the vodka bottle deep into the cornfield. But the X-ray technician at the hospital in Charlottesville told me I was drunk. I told him he was mistaken, and I later lied directly to my father about whether I had been drinking or not. No bones were broken, and the reckless-driving charge was somehow reduced to improper turn.

That spring, I dropped acid before going to my work-study job in the dean's office, and I smoked hash on the steps of the Rotunda. During a Friday-night antiwar demonstration, a group of us were chased by club-wielding state troopers in helmets, flak jackets, and gas masks. The troopers didn't catch me, but they did catch scores of others that night, including a boy trying to deliver pizza to the university president's mansion and a number of couples on their way to the Old South dance at the Kappa Alpha fraternity house. The arrested girls wore high heels and pastel gowns with hooped skirts. They cried as they were led off to jail.

In the meantime, I thought I'd found someone to replace Claire Miller. Her name was Danner. She was a senator's daughter who went to Hollins College, and on the night the ROTC building at Virginia burned, she and I lay naked in my bed listening to the sirens and watching the shadowy light from the distant flames dance against the bedroom wall. I figured we ought to be making love, but Danner was a virgin and I didn't want to press her on this point. It was enough to just lie there at the center of what we thought was a revolution and watch the shadows on the wall.

On my last trip to Virginia, to pack up my belongings after graduation, I showed up drunk at Claire Miller's door to announce that I was on my way to Vietnam to get myself killed. I volunteered for the draft, but the Army stationed me at Fort Polk, Louisiana, instead of Vietnam. Halfway through my tour, I married a girl from Birmingham named Susan McCarn. She had been a literature student at Birmingham-Southern College, where I sometimes hung out with friends, and she, too, was coming off a broken romance. Susan had been wild in college, my friends told me, something of an anarchist, or at least with that look—straight-legged jeans, chestnut hair cropped like a boy's, an intense outrage in her eyes as she argued across booths in the student snack bar. I grew to love her for exactly those qualities, and for the fact that she liked Keats and hated Republicans. We shared a dream of reading books and going to England together someday. For the time being, though, we lived off-post in De Ridder, Louisiana, in an upstairs garage apartment, and occasionally, when I threw up blood after a night of Scotch and cheap wine, Susan had to take me to the emergency room.

After the Army, I went to graduate school at the Iowa Writers' Workshop. I drank a lot, wrote a few new stories, and started what would later become a novel about a de-formed boy looking for his father, an unconscious attempt, through the terrible truth of fiction, to find a way to believe again in the God of my childhood, the one who was always just around the bend in the creek, where the mockingbirds nested and the water snakes lay tangled in a silent heap.

I drove a bus to help pay my tuition at Iowa, mostly the night shift. But sometimes, even on the day shift, I left the bus running at a stop and ran into a bar for a quick one before continuing the route. I also delivered the *Des Moines Register*. The papers arrived before dawn, and some-times I'd be too hungover to deliver them, or I wouldn't be home from drinking yet, and Susan, who worked the all-night shift as a cashier at a grocery store, would have to deliver the papers for me.

Before class, my teacher, Raymond Carver, and I would meet at a bar for drinks. Sometimes we even had class in the bar. After class we stayed out all night drinking. When Ray ate with Susan and me, we'd station a fifth of vodka on the kitchen counter especially for him. He had us over to his apartment for dinner. He didn't have any silverware or plates, though, so we passed around a bottle of vodka and ate Hamburger Helper out of Ray's skillet, using the same fork.

Susan and I moved back to Birmingham after graduate school, and that's when I met up with Vicki again, in the summer of 1975. I'm sure I had seen her a number of other times over the years, in one context or another—certainly at her brother Randy's wedding, shortly before my own, in the spring of 1971. But this time I truly saw her. Vicki was twenty-two. I was twenty-six. I had been married for four years, and now I was teaching at a small black college and acting in plays that Randy directed at Birmingham Festival Theatre.

Vicki will tell you that the crucial moment occurred when she took me into a darkened bedroom of Randy's house above the Highlands Golf Course and kissed me. I remember that moment, of course. But I think the seed of what was to happen between us was planted either right before the kiss or right afterward, as we stood in the laundry room, away from the party, and simply talked to one another at length for the first time ever. I don't remember what we talked about. It's the tone I remember, the quietness, the slowly evolving astonishment. We seemed to know each other in ways that we couldn't have. I felt like I was talking to her in my true voice, which I hadn't heard in years. And what she said to me in return was a form of physical relief, like food or water or sleep.

We have photos from that night. In one of them, I am sitting in Vicki's lap on the sofa. It is not a lewd pose. It seems to me to be filled with a sense of comfort and solidarity. Just before the photo was taken, we had made a pact to become lovers. Soon after that night, we did. There were no games between us then, no world other than the one we would create together.

The first time I went to her apartment, we smoked a joint and had a drink, vodka on ice with a slice of lime. She asked if she could take off her shirt. Then we lay down together on her bed, which had a blue spread and a view of the lights of the city. There was a lit candle on the bedside table, in honor, we decided, of Bastille Day.

To this day, I love the way Vicki smells. When we were having our affair more than twenty years ago, I would let myself into her apartment when she wasn't there. I would shamelessly read what she'd written in her journals, and then I would go to the closet in her bedroom and gather her clothes into my arms so that I could smell her in them. I wanted to wear Vicki, to put her on, the way one might a full body suit. I wanted to be totally inside her, my head, torso, arms and legs. I wanted to wear her hands and fingers like gloves. When we'd venture out on my motorcycle, we felt like the city belonged to us. We thought of ourselves as outlaws.

In the summer of 1976 I got a job teaching at a college in Ohio. It seemed a natural point of departure. Susan and I decided to separate, and I moved to Ohio alone.

Once, when Vicki came up to see me, I had a vision. I thought we were Adam and Eve. It was below zero outside, but the Garden was in our bed, and I knew we were supposed to be fruitful and live our lives together as though we were the first and only man and woman on earth and civilization depended on us. After everything that's happened, I still believe that.

war zones

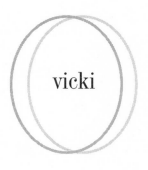

vicki

It was the fall of 1977, and we weren't married yet. We were living in Wooster, Ohio, a typical college town located in the heart of Midwestern farm country, where Dennis had landed a job at the College of Wooster. The architecture of the place was Victorian, for the most part, and Dennis and I were house-sitting for a professor on sabbatical in England. I wasn't able to find a job in mental health, so I worked as a waitress at a coffee shop, where my Southern accent was a novelty but didn't get me big tips. On breaks I sat at a table smoking Merit Menthol 100's, staring at people. They wore dark coats and talked in clips. I might as well have been in Tanzania, so massive was my culture shock. Maybe it was the pot. It was "homegrown," and I didn't know if this meant it was from Ohio or Michigan or Indiana or Iowa. It tasted different from the stuff back in Alabama that was supposedly from the Caribbean.

Sometimes I had anxiety attacks at Buehler's Market and had to flee, leaving behind a grocery cartful of eggs, bread, fruit, milk, cheese, and beer. I'd get right up to the cash register and pull out my checkbook, but when I saw the address by my name—2056 Cleveland Road, Wooster, Ohio—I went into bona fide panic, ran to my Chevy Nova in the parking lot, and drove quickly to Babcock Hall at the college, where Dennis was stuffed away in a dank basement office meant to drive men mad so they'd leave academia before coming up for tenure and thereby spare the department the ensuing battle and pay raise. I found him at his desk wearing jeans and looking like he'd just been thrown from a bull in a rodeo, and I fell in love all over again and remembered why I was living there in the first place.

I sat by his desk and said, "I had a panic attack in the grocery store." The left lens of Dennis's wire-rims was shattered from a rock that his motorcycle had kicked up.

He grabbed his helmet as if I'd just informed him that I'd had a seizure and needed CPR, and we jumped on his Honda 500T and flew past the college library, the administration building, and on down to the Nold Avenue Bar on the very edge of town. It was a blue-collar tavern by the railroad tracks, surrounded by grain elevators and a junkyard with big pieces of equipment—dies for presses that made car parts. The sight of metal was comforting. It reminded me of Birmingham.

Sometimes we drank alone, but most of the time we drank with Dennis's best friend, Stan. Stan was a big man who taught Latin American Studies. When he talked to you, he was intense, nailing you with his blue eyes, breathing hard as if in hot pursuit of some part of you.

One evening we met him at the Nold. All the regulars were there. Antoine, who got drunk every night because his wife had been killed in a house fire when he was drunk, and who felt so guilty he had to keep drinking. Ellie, the bartender. The Rubbermaid workers—Wooster was the home of Rubbermaid, Inc. When night began to fall, Dennis pulled a joint from the cellophane part of his cigarette pack. Stan waved it away. He didn't like pot. Dennis and I went to the parking lot to smoke. It was getting dark, but I could see a few train cars on the track beside the steel presses at the plant across the street.

"I'm homesick," I told him.

He hugged me, and I put my hands under his leather jacket. I liked his body—the lean, raw-boned feel of it. I liked his boots. I liked that he was one of my brother's friends.

But I didn't like Ohio.

"I hate this place," I told Stan when we went back inside the bar. The lens of Dennis's shattered glasses made a spiderweb in the jukebox light.

"Can you see with those things?" Stan asked him.

"It's kind of like tripping," Dennis said. "But it's all right."

"We don't like to fix things," I reminded Stan. I leaned over to him. "Don't you think Dennis is like one of those flossy dogs that's half-crazed from too much inbreeding, like a golden retriever or a cocker spaniel, galloping aimlessly through life?"

Stan pushed back, considering. But he didn't answer me. He just stared at us.

I held his gaze. He was of Swedish ancestry—strongly framed, almost bigger than both Dennis and me put together.

He offered us a Camel. It wasn't our brand, but we took one anyway.

We played Linda Ronstadt's "Blue Bayou" over and over.

I'm going back someday, come what may
To Blue Bayou.

"I'm going back," Stan said, but I knew he didn't have anywhere to go back to. He was from Pennsylvania. He'd gotten a Ph.D. at the University of Michigan. He wanted to be Southern, though; he'd said so, more than once.

He wanted something we had.

"What makes me like whiskey so much?" I asked.

"You're Irish, baby," Dennis said, and grinned over at me. Then he looked across the table at Stan. "She's Cherokee, too." Stan glanced at my cheekbones, then searched my eyes.

We had another round of drinks.

Dennis and Stan talked about how they hated academic life, how bad the pay was, Stan's trip last summer to Central America. Occasionally Stan broke into Spanish. He taught us to say *sucio*, which meant "dirty"; *puta*, which meant "whore"; and *chíngate*, which meant "screw you." This all seemed eminently important.

We sat at the Nold getting drunk, and when we finally got in my Nova to drive home, I sat in the middle, between them. We drove away from the steel presses and railroad tracks. We passed the campus and Buehler's Market.

"That's where I panicked," I noted.

We stopped at the liquor store, got a bottle of 151 rum, and drove on to Cleveland Road. The dog who lived at the house we were renting met us at the back door, barking like

66

crazy. He was a high-strung mutt, but I loved him madly. He was like a seeing-eye dog.

I went to the kitchen and fixed us some 151 on the rocks. It never for a moment entered my mind that we were all alcoholics. We were *desperados*. I took the drinks to Dennis and Stan, who were on the sofa. I gave them their 151 and sat in a Martha Washington chair by the fireplace. Dennis informed us that he was seeing an angel in the marble.

"Really," he said, his eyes narrowing. "I can see her."

Stan looked at me.

Dennis tilted his head to the side. "She's moving," he said, of his angel. "She's big."

And then it was silent.

"When is it going to happen?" I asked.

It wasn't so cryptic a question. The erotic tension had been gathering steam all night and even before. It was fueled by liquor and the fact that it was 1977, when anything was possible and most things were probable, sexually speaking. Stan shrugged, and Dennis rolled his cigarette in the ashtray until the hot ashes formed a point.

I don't know how to make this artful, because it wasn't. We were drunk. We moved, the three of us, from the living room up the stairs. It was dark, and we didn't get under the covers. We had talked about doing this, and now it was going to happen.

It did happen.

Dennis and I were always wanting to take somebody else along for the ride. We needed a sidekick. We needed a buddy. We were always drawing a friend in as if we were running a pyramid business and were looking for recruits. This would take many forms over the years, some of them noble, like seducing friends into going along on mission trips to Central America. But for a long, long time, it only wreaked havoc.

Stan left at some point during the night. I woke up the next morning beside Dennis. We looked at each other. It was a familiar scenario, one that all drunks know well. What had we done? Had anybody been hurt? Hit? Pushed? Taken to the hospital? Arrested? We didn't talk about what had happened. We just got up, threw on some jeans, and went downstairs. I let the dog out and smoked a cigarette while he raced all over the yard, tromping on what was left of the vegetable garden.

Weeks later, Dennis and I sat by the fireplace where he'd seen the angel. "She was the angel of death," he said. "Like you," he added, looking at me and in me and through me and beyond me, all at once. We were arguing about Stan, about whose idea it had been to have a threesome. I was denying it was mine. But Dennis was going to extract the truth like a tooth. He was going to pry it from me, to cut flesh if need be. He had secured the proper instrument for the procedure, a tape recorder.

"The truth," Dennis kept saying, putting the microphone in my face. We went upstairs to the back bedroom, where Dennis often wrote at a white desk that faced the vegetable garden. We went in and out of all the rooms, and I shuddered to think of a family, a real family, living in this place where we were fighting this ignoble fight. The rooms were cold and dusty, with dark walls. "The truth," he kept saying, forcing the tape recorder on me, shoving the microphone closer and closer to my mouth, until he finally jammed it in. If you look closely enough, you can, to this day, see where a tiny bit of tooth was chipped. I can run my tongue over it, seeking and finding the place.

After we got the fight out of the way, Dennis put his hand through the bedroom window, and I took him to the emergency room. They saw him quickly since he was bleeding a lot—there had been a storm window behind the regular window—but he refused to let them sew his hand up until they could assure him that this country would someday have national health insurance. It was a predicament for the doctors and nurses. They came out to speak with me about it.

"Where does he work?" they asked me.

"At the college," I told them.

They looked at one another, raised an eyebrow or two. The resident on call toyed with his stethoscope and after a while put a hand under his chin, surveying me. "What does he *teach*?" he asked.

"Writing," I told him.

He nodded and went back through the swinging doors. I walked in and saw Dennis in one of the rooms.

"Hey, baby," he said.

The standoff went on a long time. Dennis was relentless in his insistence on a promise from the medical staff. No national health insurance, no sutures. Simple as that. In time, he gave in, or perhaps some nurse jerked some sense into him, but we did, at some juncture, head for the door—with sutures. The resident stopped us in the ER hallway and asked where we lived.

"A few blocks away," we told him.

He lowered his voice. "I suggest you walk," he said. "There's a policeman standing right over there, and he's waiting to arrest you if you get in the car."

I had recently gotten a job as a counselor. I ran DUI groups at a mental health center. We took the resident's advice and walked. We held hands all the way home. The night was crisp. Things were looking up. But when we walked into the kitchen, we discovered that we had polished off the 151. I stared at the empty bottle. This wasn't good. We didn't have a car, and we didn't have any liquor, and the night was young. After an hour or so, we walked back to the hospital parking lot. We surveyed the place for cops. We didn't see any, so we got in my Nova and headed for Dino's Drive-Thru, where we bought a case of beer. After all, it had been a bad night. It was enough to make a person want a drink.

Later, when we got in bed, Dennis turned to me. I could make out, in the dark, the face of the man I loved—the angular, Appalachian bone structure. The wistful eyes.

He was a drunk. So was I.

But even in the worst moments, and that night ranks, I knew there was something good in us. You get a deck of genetic cards. If you carry the gene that makes you want to self-destruct, it will play. But even when it's playing, even when it's killing you, you're under there somewhere, vulnerable and worthwhile—so very worthwhile.

A few months after the incident with Stan, I got out of bed one night, went downstairs, turned on a lamp, and picked up an issue of *The New Yorker*. There was a Laurie Colwin story called "The Lone Pilgrim." The last two paragraphs went like this:

You long for someone to love. You find him. You pine for him. Suddenly, you discover you are loved in return. You marry. Before you do, you count up the days you spent in other people's kitchens, at dinner tables, putting other people's children to bed. You have basked in a sense of domesticity you have not created but enjoy. The Lone Pilgrim sits at the dinner parties of others, partakes, savors, and goes home in a taxi alone.

Those days were spent in quest—the quest to settle your own life, and now the search has ended. Your imagined happiness is yours. Therefore, you lose your old bearings. On the one side is your happiness and on the other is your past—the self you were used to, going through life alone, heir to your own experience. Once you commit yourself, everything changes and the rest of your life seems to you like a dark forest on the property you have recently acquired. It is yours, but still you are afraid to enter it, wondering what you might find: a little chapel, a stand of birches, wolves, snakes, the worst you can imagine, or the best . . .

My parents grew up in Hueytown, Alabama, a small Southern town built on dangerous occupations like mills, mines, and racing—home of many notable NASCAR drivers. My mother kept a journal of their courtship, and for this reason I know the details. They met on February 17, 1937. My dad was wearing a sweatshirt with Tom Mix on it, riding his horse and swinging a lasso in the air. My mother was wearing a red-print dress and oxfords. According to her journal, they were too shy to speak for almost a year. In the summer of

1938, Daddy came to see her for the first time, and a year later they started dating. They sat by the fire, talked, and went to the kitchen to make sandwiches. After they graduated from high school in 1941, Daddy went to the University of Alabama and Mother went to work for the telephone company. They'd planned to get married, but the war began and all the cards were suddenly in the air. In July 1943 Daddy joined the Navy and was placed in New Haven, Connecticut, to attend Yale under the U-12, a naval program that assigned enlistees to educational programs. It was merely chance that he was directed to an Ivy League school and arrived there, a country boy from Alabama, still saying, "He don't" and "She don't." But he was smart. He learned standard English grammar, majored in metallurgical engineering, and lettered in baseball. Mother worked at the phone company in Birmingham and made enough money to attend the University of Alabama for a few sessions at a time. At midnight on October 22 (which would be my birthday), he gave her an engagement ring. Daddy graduated from Yale in 1944 at the tender age of nineteen, then went straight into midshipmen's school at Columbia. The next fall he came home and married my mother. In the wedding photo my father wears his Navy uniform and my mother wears flowers in her hair. Her mouth is opening as if she's ready to speak.

I was reminded of the photograph as I stood there in their living room thirty-four years later, getting married in a hippie dress that laced up the front like a shoe. I had studied that picture a lot over the years. It was as if there were some truth embedded in their faces, some clue as to who I was and what marriage was. Or maybe I just wanted to stare at their youthful faces and ask: If you knew what lay ahead, would you still be smiling? If you knew just how different you are; how you, Daddy, will demand order and tradition; and how you, Mother, will try to escape it?

After the wedding, Dennis and I returned to Ohio.

One morning that winter, he came downstairs wearing his Army jacket. The zipper pull had broken off, so he kept a fork in his pocket to snag the mechanism in order to zip it. We stood in the kitchen, trying to figure out what to do. Hangovers had a way of making us want to go somewhere, to travel the distance. Back in autumn, we had driven to Niagara Falls on a hungover whim and the transmission in my Nova had died, leaving us stranded in North Tonawanda, New York, where my parents graciously—oh, the grace of my parents; God grant me the willingess to extend it to my own children—wired us $500 without asking questions. "Don't worry," my mother had said, "we were going to give you this money anyway for a wedding gift."

We didn't want to venture far this time. We didn't want another Niagara Falls.

"Amish country," Dennis said, tossing his cigarette into the shrubs.

The largest Amish community in the United States lies south of Wooster. If you take County Road 83 to Millersburg, you will see the telephone lines disappear. That is the first sign. In time, you see a black buggy, and if you're lucky, you catch a glimpse of an Amish girl, the aqua curtains that mark the home, a potato field, a silo.

We smoked a joint, and Dennis maneuvered the back roads perfectly, taking us deeper and deeper. He always had a nose for the meat of things. We didn't say much. I rolled the window down and tossed the last of the joint. Dennis pulled off the road and parked the car near a stand of blue spruce. We were in a neighborhood of sorts, only the houses were set apart by fields of tobacco, corn, and wheat.

In the distance was what looked like a big russet barn. "A rich Amish man must own that," I commented.

When we got to it, Dennis opened the big sliding door. Inside was a long granary, crisscrossed with shafts of light. A man's big-rimmed black hat hung on one wall. The floor was covered with straw and the walls were flecked with chaff. The smell of timothy hay was strong.

"It's a threshing den," Dennis said.

Alfalfa bales were stacked behind wooden benches that lined the back of the barn, where a cross was nailed to the wall.

"It's a church, too," I said.

I was uncomfortable. In spite of all the things Dennis and I talked about, spirituality was off limits. His first wife, Susan, had made him do the church-wedding thing, and I didn't want to be like her. I wanted to be the Cosmic Cowgirl. I wanted to drink whiskey and be cynical. I thought bawdiness was what he loved about me, so I nurtured it, and this moment of vulnerability in the threshing den, this holy silence, caught me off guard.

We sat on a pew.

I had brought along a book I found in the place we were house-sitting. It was called *Amish Society*, and in the introduction was a passage that read: *The Amish view of reality is conditioned by a dualistic world view. Light and truth coexist with the powers of darkness and falsehood. Purity and good are in conflict with impurity and evil.*

I considered for a moment. I did have a concept of right and wrong. My father had taught me absolutes: It is right to go to church. It is wrong to sleep in on Sundays. It is right to save. It is wrong to spend. It is right to be faithful. It is wrong to commit adultery.

My mother's laws were easier: Love everybody, play in the dirt, and dress like you want to dress. If Dennis was born to a man who liked to dance and a woman who didn't, maybe it's safe to say that I was born to a man who wanted to do right and a woman who wanted to do what she wanted to do. I've often wondered if I am, as a result, a bad girl trying to be good or a good girl trying to be bad.

I attached what was left of the last joint to a roach clip.

"Listen to this," I said. "*Women should spend time doing good instead of taking care of canaries, goldfish, or house flowers.*"

I passed him the joint. He took a draw of it and commented that we might want to get a canary. I reminded him that I was scared of birds.

We didn't say much more. I simply remember it as the moment when I was first aware that we couldn't talk about spiritual matters, in a place that begged for it.

After a while, we got into the car. We drove through the outlying towns—Walnut Creek, Berlin, Winesburg, Charm. We saw farmers gathering loose stones from the fields, girls in bonnets playing on a wagon, a schoolhouse here and there. When we were almost to Wooster, just as we came over the crest of a hill, we saw that an Amish buggy had been hit by a car. The driver wasn't hurt, but the buggy was overturned and a wheel was separated from the carriage. The horse was on its side, and it was injured. What would they do, I wondered, since they didn't believe in guns or vets? The accident bothered me more than I wanted it to. We might so easily have been the drivers of the car.

We survived the winter of 1977–78, then decided to call it quits and move back to Birmingham. Stan helped us pack up. He cried most of the day while we crammed everything we owned into my rusty Nova. I put all my underwear in a plastic trash bag, and since the car was packed to the hilt, we tied the trash bag to the luggage rack. We had just crossed the Ohio River, from Cincinnati into Covington, Kentucky, when the trash bag exploded. I watched all my underwear fly into the wind and scatter along the interstate.

After I lost the underwear, I never looked back.

When we got home to Birmingham, we rented a one-bedroom apartment on Southside. The apartment was cut at an angle that allowed for a fireplace, but the entire square footage couldn't have been more than three hundred feet. I got a job working with criminals in a drug-rehab program, and Dennis taught part-time and wrote short stories. He turned thirty. We cut back on liquor.

In the summer of 1979, we stopped using birth control. We rode the train to New Orleans in the fall. Dennis took a picture of me there, and when it was developed, it showed me peering sideways into the lens as if doubting life's sincerity. I had a dream while we were in New Orleans. A woman said to me, "Look in your mind's eye. If October 4 falls on a Thursday, you'll understand it when it happens." I wrote the dream in my journal, but I didn't check the date, because we were on a trip and I didn't have a calendar handy.

We rode the train back to Birmingham, and before we could get the film developed, I learned I was pregnant. For a few days I floated along in bliss. I'm normal, I thought. I'm going to have a baby. I'm a normal person. I had never, ever thought of myself in this way. But a month later I started bleeding. I went to the doctor, and he told me I was probably miscarrying. They did a sonogram, and there was no baby in my uterus. So I went into the hospital for a D&C.

A few days later I was walking down the apartment stairs to get the mail, running my hands along the white banister. Suddenly a jolt of pain broke me in two. It almost had noise to it, like a tree branch snapping. I made it back up the stairs, went into the apartment, and lay down on the bed. I was wearing jeans and I unzipped them because my belly felt distended. I lay there awhile, and then I tried to get up, but when I did, I felt so dizzy I lay back down. I couldn't go anywhere or do anything because I knew I'd pass out if I moved.

Dennis came home.

"Something's wrong," I told him.

He didn't ask questions. He just called the doctor. He later told me my face was gray, set like stone. I told him my shoulder was hurting. He told the doctor this. The doctor said to come to the emergency room. I later learned that the shoulder pain was deferred pain, a classic symptom of the awful thing that was happening to me. On the ride to the hospital I was as sublime as I'd ever been in my life, sailing on endorphin zaniness. The sky was tinged with October red. We got to the ER, and I made it to a bed. Triage gave me secondary status, but after a while I pled with the nurse to do something.

"I can't zip my jeans," I told her.

She looked at me as if this was comical in its irrelevance.

When the doctor arrived, he said, "I'm going to have to put a needle in your vagina to see if there is blood." The violation was beyond anything my mind was willing to accept, and I grabbed the nurse and jerked her body to my chest. She let me. She let herself be used by me. She absorbed my pain. I would always remember this. Twenty years later, I remember knowing at that moment in 1979 what I know today: All I ever wanted in life was a baby.

That nurse knew it, too.

They took me to emergency surgery and gave me a spinal, since I had eaten within the last few hours. "This is an ectopic pregnancy," a nurse told me. "The baby has been growing in your Fallopian tube rather than your uterus. The baby has gotten big enough to rupture the tube."

The reason I couldn't zip my jeans was that too much blood was oozing into my abdomen. They gave me a narcotic. "Is your shoulder better now?" somebody asked me. The operating room was cold and everything was silver—the tables, the instruments, the taste in my mouth.

A nurse sat near my head.

The table shook with the movements of the instruments, and I thought, They've got my body cut open. I threw up. Before long, my mind started throwing up. I'd had this feeling on LSD.

A surgeon was whistling. There were a lot of people in the room, and some of them were talking about being late for supper. I didn't understand what they were doing, but after a while Dr. Lewis—my gynecologist at the time—said, "We're just taking one tube. We're leaving both ovaries."

He was trying to assure me that I still had a chance for another baby, but I didn't assimilate the meaning of anything. I was struggling for equilibrium.

Later, I looked at the calendar and saw that October 4 was on a Thursday, as the voice in my dream had predicted. That was the day I lost the baby. For a brief time I felt spiritual. I'd almost died, and I was grateful to God, though I didn't know exactly who He was, and I certainly didn't want to actually *change* anything about myself, be a better person. I did want something from Him, though. I had started reading the bad odds of ever having a baby after an ectopic in which the tube ruptures.

I wanted God to give me a baby.

I believed that if I believed in Him, if I believed He gave a damn about me, He'd give me what I wanted. In that sense, I began thinking of Him in a more personal way. I'd grown up in a Baptist church where spirituality was a legalistic matter. My mother, though, had other ideas. She had tried to teach me that it's all about love and wonder, not fear and guilt. The church should be more concerned with meeting needs than making rules. I had a need. "God *cares* for you," my mother said in that lyrical way of hers. Since it came from her, I thought maybe He did. If only He was a mother, not a father. A mother would certainly allow me to conceive again.

We moved from the apartment into a house on Green Springs Avenue. I planted a garden, and we got a golden retriever named Ellie. I entered fertility treatment. I didn't get pregnant, but Ellie did. She gave birth to eight puppies, and we kept the blond, female runt. We named her Annie.

I wrote short stories.

But I wanted a baby. Only those who have struggled know the intensity of this longing, the biological imperative that makes you run to the clinics, spend the money, cajole desire according to the peaks and valleys on the temperature chart, all the while wondering if you'll ever be able to be sexually spontaneous again.

You won't.

In the South, we have family doctors. The specialist I went to first was the oldest, most respected gynecologist in Birmingham. He had been a friend of my father since childhood, and I was among his second-generation patients. He had Jack Benny's dry wit, and he was also very direct. I told him I'd had an ectopic pregnancy.

"You had the Copper 7 IUD?" he guessed, correctly.

"Yes," I replied.

"You know it's not just IUDs that scar the tubes and cause ectopics," he told me. I looked into the blue of his eyes. I knew what was coming.

"It's pelvic inflammatory disease," he went on.

I nodded.

"Promiscuity is a culprit," he concluded.

I didn't take it as a scolding. I knew he was leveling with me. He gave me a temperature chart, and I kept it religiously. The ovulation peak was like a church steeple, so perfectly defined, as if my body had form and dignity.

After a year of trying to make love on the right days, I still hadn't conceived. The OB suggested adhesions as a probable diagnosis, and he performed microsurgery on my remaining Fallopian tube. It was a success, and I left the hospital ready to get pregnant. I didn't, and so after another year I went to a clinic at the medical center. The obstetrical side was a swarm of lower-socio-stratum women with babies galore. The infertility side was a quiet sanctuary of professional women like myself. I liked the specialist well enough to give it a run. I repeated the temp charts and did the other tests, too. Dennis's sperm count was good. Under the microscope, they scurried like tiny tadpoles. I feared this was all I'd ever see of a baby, and it was his part, swimming madly—like Dennis himself—searching for a part of me.

In Radiology, I undressed under dim lights that threw a lavender tint on my skin. I flexed a muscle and thought how a woman's skeletal structure was supposed to be perfect at age thirty. But I felt out of sync with myself, and it scared me to think the infertility might be psychogenic in nature, somehow related to the women on my father's side of the family, who were passionate to a fault. One of them, a kind and drunk and beautiful lesbian, had shot herself on a sailboat. Her life story was family lore.

"Remember Reba," I'd often hear someone warn if I ever hinted of being depressed or wanting to sail.

The specialist entered the room, his face cherubic as he hooked my feet in the stirrups. "I'm going to dilate and inject dye," he said, displaying a big needle that reminded me of the one they put in me to diagnose the ectopic. "We'll see if there's still tubal blockage."

"I've had surgery to fix that," I reminded him.

"Yes," he replied, flipping the chart. The pain of the needle was a tiny gunshot. On a TV screen I watched dye run and loop over in nice arcs.

"What's that?" I asked, pointing to a dark place that looked like a kidney bean.

"Your cervix."

When it was all done, I went back to his office and he moved his hands oddly, as if shaping an invisible ball of clay. I knew he was going to deliver bad news.

"It looks like your sole Fallopian tube is badly damaged on the fimbrial end," he said. "By fimbrial I mean the end with the fingers," he clarified, and waved his own fingers like so many snakes.

I waited.

Sometimes you don't ask the big question.

"You want odds," he went on, knowing that, of course, I did want odds. I was almost thirty years old and I had a master's degree and I wanted odds.

"Maybe 10 percent of ever conceiving," he told me.

I walked to my car, and a flock of transient birds stopped to light in a shedding oak. I stood under the tree for a moment, and then I went home to Dennis.

No baby?

Then let's wreck the nest.

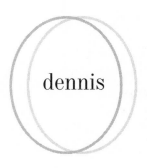

dennis

When I was a boy, I belonged to the Air Force Club. It was founded by Generals Joe Potter and Butch Fike. Leonard Gavin was a major. The rest of us were enlisted men. We conducted maneuvers in the cauliflower field down the alley from my house. We dug foxholes in our yards and threw dough balls wrapped in newspaper because they marked kills better than mud. We practiced parachuting off the roof of the toolshed in Joe Potter's back yard. The shed was stuffed with discarded airplane parts, pieces of cockpit instrument panels, and scraps of wire and brass we'd picked up at Saturday-morning salvage sales at Hayes Aircraft. Sometimes we conducted court-martials in my basement. I was never court-martialed, but I did get busted once, from sergeant to corporal, for quitting a hike to the colored cemetery so that I wouldn't be late for my piano lesson.

Eventually we got into rocketry, and the end for me came when we were challenged to wage war against the Navy Club, commanded by Leonard Gavin's cousin Danny Trotman, who lived on the other side of Division Avenue, a world away. I pleaded with my father, but I was younger than the other boys, and it was the one thing he wouldn't let me do. So the Air Force Club went to war without me. In the confusion of battle, one of our smoke bombs burned down the Trotmans' garage. I rarely questioned my father's judgment after that.

But I worried that a real war might not come along in time for me. When it finally did, I didn't want to go to it anymore. It was 1970, the first year of the military draft lottery. My college roommates and I watched the drawing on TV. My birthday was one of the unlucky ones, number 32. Since the draft was going to get me anyway, I volunteered. I did my basic training at Fort Polk, Louisiana. After basic I was assigned the job classification 11B, which meant my next stop was advanced infantry training (AIT) at North Fort, the quickest route to Vietnam. But there was only one moment when I really thought I was going.

I was lying in my bunk at North Fort in the middle of a two-week leadership-preparation course prior to AIT. Because I was a college boy, I'd been chosen as acting sergeant for my platoon, but I knew I hadn't been doing things right. I was too friendly with my subordinates, and I often got into political arguments with our instructors, Vietnam combat veterans who were in no mood to entertain smart-asses like me.

That night, though, I was convinced I was going to war. I wrote a letter to my parents, a wry, stiff-upper-lip kind of farewell, and then I lay in the dark and watched the shadows of trees through the screen window of my barracks. The air was moving, and the world seemed very large and ominous. I had an unreasonable but palpable fear that my life had been orchestrated for just this moment. I would be sent to Vietnam. I would be killed. It would be my punishment for wanting to go to war so badly when I was a boy.

But the next day I barked out a cadence wrong. My instructor was suddenly screaming at me. He was shorter than I was, with a round, perpetually red face. He unpinned the sergeant's stripes from my fatigue shirt and told me I didn't have what it took to be a platoon leader. I'd go to Vietnam, all right, he said, but it would be as a common grunt.

I spent the rest of the leadership-preparation course picking up cigarette butts, weeding, emptying trash cans. Then the commanding officer called me into his quarters. A legal unit on post needed a court reporter, he said. He'd been looking at my records, and I qualified. Did I want the job?

Did I want the job? I remember running down the sidewalk after telling him yes. I remember leaping into the air and literally clicking my heels together. But I remember, too, even at the apex of my joy, the shadow of an unsettling notion—that I might not have to go to Vietnam after all, and that I might miss something important there.

Novelist Tim O'Brien says, "I was a coward. I went to Vietnam." I suppose I understand what he means, in a political sense, but I still feel the courageous thing would have been to go, as O'Brien did, if called. Of course, it's an easy thing for me to say now. I was never called.

Instead, I led that slothful, Stateside existence of too much

marijuana and too many drive-in movies, too many enchi-
ladas and absolutely no women. My Army buddies were
Dimitrios Zangos, a Greek artist; John Hall, a North Carolina
truck driver; and Felix Ramos, a Chicano intellectual. We
cultivated friendships with the post military police, who sup-
plied all the good drugs. We avoided the drunks and the
heroin addicts in our barracks, and stuck to immense quantities of good weed and an occasional hit of acid. I think
Ramos, though, stayed straight. Every morning the rest of us
met in the woods behind the barracks to get stoned. Sometimes we'd slip out before dawn and go bass fishing at Bun-
dick Lake. On weekends we'd take road trips—to Houston,
so Zangos could show us the art museum; to Lake Charles,
so we could spend five minutes apiece dancing with a Cajun
girl on a floor crowded with lonely soldiers like us. But mostly
we just talked about heavy things—art, politics, life.

All in all, it wasn't such a bad time, and I started to worry
that I might prefer the company of men to that of women.
But I kept writing poems and sending them to Susan McCarn,
the last woman I'd dated in Birmingham. She wrote me back,
enclosing favorite poems of her own, especially those of John
Donne, George Herbert, and Matthew Arnold, and on
Christmas leave, she picked me up at the bus station in downtown Birmingham.

It is late, a frigid December night. Susan and I are walking
to her car in an eerie half-light, the air filled with the acrid
smell of smoke. It's more than the usual stench of the steel
mills. It's as though the entire city is on fire, and when we
round a corner, we see that the Lawrence Furniture store,
across from the Alabama Theater on Third Avenue North, is

burning down. The fire trucks have all arrived, and the fire-
men are busy hosing the roofs of adjoining buildings from
their hook and ladders, but the flames from the furniture-
store fire rise high above them into the night sky.

We stop to watch. I'm wearing my dress greens and carrying my AWOL bag. "There's an awful beauty to it, isn't
there?" Susan says. That's when I know I am going to ask
her to marry me.

My Army buddies were stunned and furious when I got
back to Louisiana.

"Why would you want to do something like that?" Zangos
said. "You don't even know the girl."

"Sure I do."

"Yeah," Hall said, blowing a marijuana smoke ring into
the air. "So how come you've never talked about her till
now?"

I looked to the back seat for support, but Ramos was not
paying attention to the conversation. We were watching *Ring
of Bright Water* at the Leesville drive-in, a family movie about
pet otters, and Ramos had his hand over his mustache, hiding
a smile at some insight he had just had, probably about the
vacuity of American domestic life.

I turned back to the movie. Zangos and Hall had a point,
but I was determined. It was my life, not theirs. I was almost
twenty-three years old. It was time. And Susan was everything I never knew I wanted—the Lake Country in autumn;
the Loch Ness monster; Wedgwood vases; Persian rugs;
physician soirees at the country club, which she disdained;
and High Church Anglicanism, which she did not. Her religious belief, though, was a source of irritation from the start.

When she told me she wanted to raise our children in the church, I replied that I'd as soon not have children at all.

Susan's mother told her I was from the wrong side of the tracks, something I couldn't dispute. Susan's father, a much-loved doctor who had died of cancer when Susan was eleven, was nobody I could compete with. I didn't want a church wedding. Susan and her mother did. I lost. But the reception was at their house, and instead of rice, our hippie friends showered Susan's new baby-blue Toyota with petals from the flowering redbud and forsythia. We spent our first night at a Holiday Inn on the road to De Ridder, Louisiana, and Susan didn't start crying until we pulled up in front of the garage apartment I'd rented for our first year of marital bliss. Zangos, Hall, and Ramos had helped me pick it out.

The thing is, that first year of marriage was, for the most part, blissful. Our shotgun apartment overlooked a fig tree in our Greek landlords' back yard. On sunny days, Mrs. Maskus hung her canary cage from one of the branches. It drove their cat bonkers. Sometimes she set up a card table beneath the tree and invited us to have coffee and pastries—baklava, almond cookies, and those mildly sweet cookies that are bent like pretzels and basted with clarified butter. I bought her husband, Charlie, cases of Pabst Blue Ribbon at the post PX. Charlie was much older than his wife, and he was always good for a story from the past. When he first came to America, he worked in a shoe factory in Massachusetts, where he said they used to celebrate Good Friday by nailing a Jewish co-worker into one of the shoe crates, and when he moved to Louisiana and saved enough money, he sent for a doe-eyed teenager he had never met who lived on the Aegean island of Lesbos, a girl who, strangely enough, wound up loving him. They had two sons, divided their garage into three apartments, and rented one of them to a newlywed couple, us.

At night Susan and I listened to Judy Collins albums and classical music on a 33-rpm record player. There was no air conditioning. The windows were open, and the air was filled with Mendelssohn and the smell of ripening figs.

This is love, I thought, not passionately messy, but gentle, hopeful, except for the alcohol and the long wait to see whether my name would come down on levy for Vietnam. It never did. Zangos became the colonel's driver and personal cartoonist. He re-upped. Hall was sent to Thailand, whence he wrote letters about exquisite women and dope. I lost track of Felix Ramos—perhaps he was the one who got sent to Vietnam—and my tour ended where it began, at Fort Polk, Louisiana, and I was the same man I was when I came in, except that I was married, and I figured I would never again have to think about going to war.

I didn't think about war again for ten years. By that time, Susan and I were divorced. Vicki and I were six years into our own marriage and living in an aging Tudor on Green Springs Avenue, our first house, but without the nursery we'd planned. Vicki loved the house. She planted a garden there and raised a litter of golden retrievers. I taught school part-time and drove a bus. We rarely argued. Both of us were writing like fiends. We would read each other's work, con-gratulate ourselves, and pour another drink.

I suppose everyone saw us as a happy couple. We hosted

birthdays and Halloween parties and family Thanksgivings on both sides. Even on regular nights, we cooked each other fantastic meals—shrimp gumbo or Mandarin beef or trout *meunière*, and in what we thought of as our best moments, we'd sit on the screened front porch and drink margaritas and smoke joints while we watched the sun set and the streetlights come on in our neighborhood.

But there was a hole at the center of our marriage, and it was bigger than the one left by Vicki's ectopic pregnancy. Our disappointment had sparked a recklessness that we saw as our revenge for childlessness. People came in and out of the house on Green Springs Avenue that year. Some of them spent the night. It was like an extended game of musical chairs. But that kind of freedom quickly lost its charm. I didn't want a party; I wanted a hiding place.

Instead of setting my house in order, I slipped away into my imagination, which had always tended more toward the romantic than the sexual. I fell for a twenty-two-year-old commercial artist with a punk haircut and irises as flat as tiddledywinks. We'd caught each other's eyes across a dance floor in the fall of 1981. Instinctively we had held up our hands, fingers splayed outward, and walked toward one another until our fingers met. She said her name was Haley. I told her mine, and then I surprised myself by asking if she was a Christian. She said yes. The music started. We danced. It seemed like we were supposed to dance.

But when we stopped for cigarettes and discovered we'd run out, Haley turned to a man I didn't know and said, "Brad, this is Dennis. We're going to run out for a pack of cigarettes."

Brad just smiled and said, "Oh no, you're not."

I went to the store alone, and when I got back, Haley and Brad were gone.

I told Vicki all about it. I didn't think for a moment I would ever see this woman again, but I did.

"So you're a love junkie," Vicki's psychiatrist told me. I wanted to hit him. Didn't he understand? I had problems living in the present. I still do. Isn't that the source of the romantic imagination, the inability to focus on the moment at hand?

I saw Haley only at times when I'd told Vicki I was seeing her. She and Brad had been married for more than a year, but he didn't know about the lunches at the park, the drinks at our local bar in the middle of the day. "I could never go to bed with a married man," Haley once told me.

Going to bed was not the issue, I wanted to say. I didn't want that any more than she did. I didn't envision us being married or having kids either. What I wanted—but how could I tell her this?—what I wanted was a walk-up apartment in the heart of Five Points South, a kitchen and one other room with off-white walls and a pair of director's chairs. What I wanted was to see Haley walk into that apartment at the end of the day and throw her bag into one of the director's chairs. I wanted us to take walks together, go to the movies, eat fruit and bread, and window-shop for clothes she liked. Simple things. That was the title of a story Vicki later wrote about a man's obsession for a girl with short cropped hair and tiny feet.

I don't know whether Haley ever loved me or not. I do believe that I loved her. But by the time she died of cancer at the age of twenty-six, it had been more than two years since she had thought of me as anything other than the source of an excruciatingly difficult friendship. She and Vicki had become close toward the end. The last time I saw Haley alive, the four of us were bowling—she and Brad, Vicki and me. On the morning a few weeks later when Vicki woke me to say that Haley had died, she also told me about the affair Haley had been having all this time with another of our friends. I didn't go to the funeral. Rage was my form of grief. I didn't know whether I was angrier at Vicki for withholding information or at Haley for dying the way she had. Whatever I had been seeking in the girl with close-cropped hair had turned out to be nothing but a deeper well of loneliness.

A defining moment: It's the stroke of midnight on New Year's Eve, 1982. I don't know why Vicki and I have begun having these New Year's Eve parties, but this one will surely be the last. Haley and Brad have left for another party. I am sitting alone in our bedroom while the chaos of the night unwinds all around me. The music is dissonant and sinister. People I don't know are setting off fireworks on the front steps. I can't see into the other rooms. I don't know where Vicki is, or with whom. I am in my own bedroom, in my own house, at the stroke of midnight on New Year's Eve, and I am utterly alone.

The next New Year's Eve, I went to Los Angeles for job interviews at the Modern Language Association convention. At midnight, I found myself looking at a partial lunar eclipse through a telescope at the Griffith Observatory, a smudge of russet against an otherwise brilliant night sky. I was more than a thousand miles from home, and the grounds of the observatory were packed with families I didn't know. But this time I wasn't alone. I had already entered into another romantic illusion. I had decided to go to El Salvador, to a war I thought would be an ultimate escape from the mess my life had become in the house without a nursery on Green Springs Avenue.

That fall I had read Michael Herr's Vietnam book, *Dispatches*, which taught me the power of literary journalism, and James Fallows's "What Did You Do in the Class War, Daddy?" which explained better than I ever could the way I felt about missing the war.

When James Fallows came to town to give a lecture, I pumped him with questions. He wrote *National Defense*, he said, out of a sense of incompleteness after having avoided the draft. I told him that I felt the same way and that I wanted to go to El Salvador. He recommended I call a friend of his, a former *New York Times* correspondent in El Salvador. The friend's advice was blunt but invaluable: "Don't go out alone. Don't go out at night. Stay at the Camino Real and stick with your fellow journalists. Remember that if you get into trouble, no Salvadoran can help you."

I figured I was going to El Salvador for the same reason others have gone to war—sometimes our spirits are led to the very places that can kill them. About that time a friend introduced me to a photographer who shared my obsession with El Salvador. Nick was younger than me, as curly-haired and impulsive as a springer spaniel. Nick and I spoke no Spanish. We'd never been to a war. I had never even been outside the U.S. or written a single word of journalism. But none of that seemed to matter now.

•   •   •

It's difficult to explain how I felt about Nick. I hardly knew him, and yet in the course of preparing for our trip to El Salvador, I had invested my trust in him. I'd asked other friends, close friends, to go with me. But Nick was the only person who said, "Let's do it." We shared the same obsession, and so we had a mordant and peculiar bond. We were using each other's enthusiasm to confer an air of normalcy and rationality on an undertaking that was clearly neither.

At night we'd sit at the bar at the Camino Real, throwing back margaritas and trying to look seasoned and unflappable, like the other journalists, mercenaries, CIA agents, and prostitutes who gathered there. Back in our room, we'd call Vicki and Nick's wife, Abby, and report the day's events with drunken, laconic bravado. If the streets outside erupted in automatic-weapons fire while we were still on the phone, we'd say, "Must have been a backfire or fireworks, that's all."

The first morning, after Nick and I got our press credentials, we met Joan Ambrose-Newton, a South African–born BBC correspondent, in the hotel elevator on our way to breakfast. "The boys have hit Tenancingo," she said. "We need warm bodies. You want to go?" Nick and I had no idea where Tenancingo was, or what exactly Joan had meant by "hit" or "warm bodies," but we grabbed our gear and followed her to the parking lot.

We took two rented cars to Tenancingo in case one broke down going in or coming out. Joan rode in the lead vehicle with another correspondent. Nick and I rode in the trailing Toyota sedan with Joe Frazier, the Associated Press bureau chief, whose wife, Linda, also a journalist, would die two years later in the bombing at La Penca, Nicaragua.

Joe Frazier knew this was our first trip into the countryside, so he tried to bring us up to speed. Tenancingo, a small town forty kilometers northeast of the capital, had been attacked and overrun by guerrillas. The Salvadoran Army garrison had been wiped out, but details were sketchy. That's why we were going there.

Frazier drove us east along the Pan-American Highway out of town, past schoolgirls in plaid skirts and boys with leashed pigs. An underpass took us beneath a runway of Ilopango airbase just as a spotter plane, probably returning from the San Vicente offensive, made its final approach for landing.

At the turnoff for Tenancingo, we stopped the cars and conferred. There was some question about whether the road into the town was mined, but when we saw truckloads of *campesinos* entering the highway from the road, we knew it was safe to continue. We passed a deserted chicken hatchery and houses with mud walls and thatched roofs. Each house had a white flag flying conspicuously out front. No one on this road could afford to take sides in the conflict.

Halfway to Tenancingo, we slowed for a knot of *campesinos*, many of them wearing sheathed machetes. They were changing a tire on a two-and-a-half-ton truck. One boy in the crowd held a dead bird in his hand. From there to Tenancingo, we didn't see a living soul, but we sensed we were drawing near town when we noticed fresh graves marked with wooden crosses along the side of the road.

The town sat on a hill, its cobbled avenues slanted inward so that sewage could flow down the middle. We pulled off to the side of the road and got out of the cars. The air was perfectly still, soundless.

"Where are the people?" Nick asked.

Joe Frazier didn't answer. "Everybody stick together and stay out in the open," he said.

We slowly made our way up the hill, stepping over piles of refuse and human excrement, discarded military boots, and empty M-16 cartridges. The low concrete buildings were bullet-pocked and covered with revolutionary slogans. In the distance, we could hear the *poc-poc* of small-arms fire and the *whump* of mortar rounds.

When we turned a corner, we saw three young men standing around a one-eared horse with splayed legs. The men appeared to be guerrillas. One was dressed in jeans, a black T-shirt, and a green felt cap. An ammunition belt was buckled around his waist, and he cradled an M-16 in the crook of his arm. Another guerrilla lounged in the doorway of a store, brooding, his shirt unbuttoned to the waist and an automatic weapon held loosely in his right hand. His boots were mismatched—one black, one brown—and the soles were separating from the uppers.

The guerrilla with mismatched boots said he'd joined the revolution five years earlier, when he was thirteen, but before he could tell us his whole story, he was interrupted by sustained bursts of automatic-weapons fire and the steady *whump whump* of mortar rounds.

Joe Frazier stopped to count the seconds between explosions. "Don't worry," he said. "They're not being walked toward us."

We followed the guerrillas into the unlighted store. Children were lined up on a bench in the shaft of light from the doorway. Some of them were naked, with distended bellies and narrow heads. A young girl picked at an open sore on one of her cheeks.

The store was bare except for two sacks of beans on the floor and two coils of rope on the counter. On the walls were advertisements for aspirin and Suprema beer, L&M and Viceroy Lights. Affixed prominently above the empty shelves was a 1982 calendar with a colored print of Jesus crowned, His hand raised in a blessing.

The guerrillas leaned their weapons against the counter while they hoisted the sacks over their shoulders and carried them outside. The woman behind the counter told us the sacks were the last of the Red Cross supplies, which were hard to come by. Sometimes the government troops wouldn't let the Red Cross deliver food to the town for fear the guerrillas would get hold of it. One day, for instance, only fifty pounds of salt got through.

The guerrillas returned for their weapons and the coils of rope. While they tied the sacks to the horse, we walked to the town square. In the city hall "Revolution or death—we shall conquer" was scrawled across a wall.

We searched for the place where the government troops had been garrisoned. An old woman pointed to a windowless aqua building with metal doors, its walls scarred by battle, particularly around the stone defenses protecting the doorways. In the street were freshly dug graves, some marked with boots and crosses made of sticks. All forty of the soldiers had been killed in the battle, the old woman said.

Inside the garrison lay the mattresses on which the troops had bedded down. Like the city hall, the place had been ransacked. Orders and morning reports covered the floor. The air was filled with flies and the smell of urine.

As we stepped back out into the thin sunlight, my eyes were drawn to the flanks of Guazapa volcano—lush, impossibly green under wisps of cloud. The sounds of battle continued incongruously in the distance.

"What can I lead with?" Joan Ambrose-Newton said. "I've written this story before."

Researchers tell us that love is more likely to spring up in dangerous situations than in ones posing no risk. In future trips to El Salvador, I would visit any number of towns like Tenancingo, and I would get much closer to the fighting itself. But Tenancingo was a turning point for me. For one thing, after Tenancingo I knew I was going to stop drinking. Those nights at the bar with the other drunks had, in ways, been more frightening than the fighting. And I began to see Vicki in a different light. All our craziness back in Birmingham had just been a way of marking time until real life came along, and there was nothing more real than the lives I was watching the Salvadorans endure, poised on the razor's edge. In ways, I fell more deeply in love with Vicki than I had ever been before. Our relationship had begun in risk, it had been tested by tragedy and carelessness, but now I missed her with the urgency that only fear can bring, the physical aching for someone you think you might never see again. I talked about Vicki incessantly after Tenancingo. I tried to explain to

Nick how much I loved her, but he didn't seem to want to hear.

When we got back to the States, we saw *The Year of Living Dangerously* together, all four of us—Vicki, Nick, Abby, and me. The movie was set in Indonesia in 1965, with Mel Gibson, Sigourney Weaver, and Linda Hunt as the hermaphroditic dwarf, Billy Kwan, the muse and moral conscience of the film. Mel Gibson was the artist as reporter, a man willing to sacrifice everything—love, God, himself—to get the story. Sigourney Weaver gave him the story he needed, and he, true writer that he was, betrayed her. In the end, though, love conquered all. A lot of people were machine-gunned along the road to the airport. Mel and Sigourney got out in the nick of time, having run roadblocks, their windshield riddled with bullets. Everybody lived happily ever after, except, one assumed, the people of Indonesia, including Billy Kwan, who fell or was pushed to his death from a seventh-story hotel room as he unfurled a sign protesting Sukarno's rule. Billy landed in the parking lot like, as Joseph Heller puts it, "a hirsute bag filled with strawberry ice cream."

It was a great flick, we all decided. It wasn't just the movie. It was the circumstances of seeing it. The movie captured precisely what Nick and I had experienced in El Salvador— the terror, the paranoia, the adrenaline high. There was an intense camaraderie among the four of us, a sense that we were the only ones in the theater who truly understood what it meant to live dangerously.

But we were manufacturing our own danger now. By the

time we saw the movie, Vicki was having an affair with Nick and I was having one with Abby. A few months later, Vicki and I stopped drinking, but the impossible had happened anyway. Vicki was pregnant. And we didn't know who the father was.

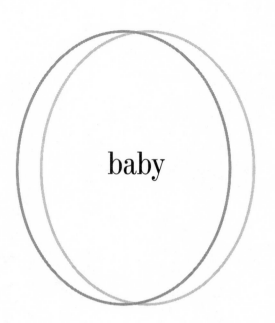

baby

vicki

Down the street and around the corner from the house on Green Springs Avenue was a bad neighborhood where big families lived in old, sagging houses that were once splendid but had been sectioned off into apartment units. In the yards, men tinkered with the undersides of rusty cars while their women drank beer and nursed babies. They were from Appalachia. You knew by the accent. Dennis liked these hill people and the raw sensuality he saw in them. I think he wanted to be like them. He wanted weeds in his yard, a walleyed child with a bouquet of dandelions, a rust-eaten car that would take him nowhere.

He was teaching part-time at night, and during the day he drove a bus for the university. We'd get up every morning at 4:30, and I'd fix him a yogurt shake in the blender and walk halfway to work with him. Then I'd head back home. When our house came into view, I'd stop and stare at it wistfully. I had wanted to buy this house very much. It reminded me of the one I grew up in, and I somehow believed that my dad might appear one Saturday morning with the old 1957 Chevy and ask me to scrub the whitewalls. The grass would turn green, a gardenia bush would spring up and prosper, and I'd be like my mother, fresh and alive.

And fertile.

I didn't become my mother, and the lawn stayed full of weeds. I did plant a vegetable garden, though, and for several summers we had a big harvest of corn, okra, tomatoes, peppers, and black-eyed peas. I kept working in substance abuse, and in 1982, Dennis started talking about Central America. I knew nothing about the region, but I could see that he was becoming intensely preoccupied—obsessed—with it. He was changing, or perhaps it's more accurate to say that a part of his makeup I'd never known was surfacing. He was cranked up, speedy, doing a hundred pushups every morning, brushing his teeth fastidiously, riding his bicycle like a madman. He'd been such a laid-back, dope-smoking hippie. Now he ricocheted between Spanish courses at the university and studying maps of war zones, especially El Salvador. He was also obsessed with a young girl named Haley who had a Peter Pan haircut and was into punk. Nothing ever came of it, but the intensity of his preoccupation with her alerted me to the fact that he was capable of extreme interests. Since I was working in mental health, I toyed with the idea that he might be bipolar. Maybe I'd seen only the depressive side, and now here was the mania emerging at last. But I knew this wasn't the correct assessment, since manic-depressives generally run on six-month cycles—up six, down six. Then, of course, there was the possibility of an obsessive-compulsive neurosis (not yet termed OCD) and attention-deficit disorder (which was, in those days, generally reserved for hyperactive kids).

We didn't use cocaine, because we never believed the kick justified the price. And though he'd loved amphetamines in college, he wasn't, I knew, into them now. So I just watched him in wonder as he darted from map to map.

The breakfast room in the house on Green Springs was painted yellow, with white woodwork. We didn't have many nice things, but the few pieces of china and stemware we did have were kept in the butler pantry, which rose up to kiss a high stucco ceiling. It was in this room that Dennis and I did a lot of drinking with Nick and Abby during the summer of 1983. Resigned bitterly to childlessness, I suddenly found all my destructive energy harnessed and viable. I crashed in on Nick like a kamikaze pilot. He had a dark side, like Dennis and me. I liked Abby, too. Her father was African, her mother Swedish—the recipe for an exotic miscegenation.

Once I knew I wanted to hook up with Nick, I started working on Dennis and Abby. I mentioned to Dennis her petulant smile. I orchestrated the dance. One day Dennis got caught in a rainstorm and hitched a ride home with her. When I saw them wet, in my kitchen, I knew they were going to be lovers. That took care of him and her.

I started calling Nick at work. I remember going over to his office building one day and asking the secretary if I might see him. It was a bold thing to do. I didn't know him outside his relationship with Dennis. I just wanted to get straight to the point: I liked him. I told him so, and as we rode the elevator back down, he looked me over with a mixture of excitement and bewilderment.

I invited Nick and Abby over. I cooked a nice dinner—

chicken in sherry, wild rice, fruit salad, homemade rolls. We ate this meal in the dining room, from the table that had belonged to my grandmother. We used cloth napkins. I deployed every Southern nicety I knew. It was a cordial, pleasant meal, until we got the whiskey out.

They spent the night.

The mutual affairs we had with them were short-lived. Nick and Abby's marriage was a house of cards already, and it fell quickly. Dennis and I didn't talk much about our relationships with them because we were caught in a terror worse than adultery. We were drinking ourselves to death, and we knew it.

That August, we went to Atlanta to a conference related to my work in the field of substance abuse. One speaker was a man from Birmingham who had gone to high school with Dennis and Randy. He was a psychiatrist, and I assumed he was going to lecture on pharmacology. Instead, he started talking about himself, about his relationship with alcohol. I told Dennis about it. We swam a few laps in the pool. We didn't drink that night or the next, but on the third day, I broke. At a restaurant I ordered a piña colada—not the usual Jack Daniel's on the rocks. I reasoned that maybe this was a "step in the right direction." Dennis had a beer. I felt relieved. I was afraid he might seriously be thinking about quitting. We had another round, but it didn't taste right. The affairs with Nick and Abby had left us sheepish and exposed, to ourselves and to each other.

A few weeks later, we went to the beach. One night we

were drinking José Cuervo under the stars. We didn't have lemon or salt, just tequila. In the distance were the lights of the ugly high-rise where we were staying. I suddenly saw it for what it was: an affront to nature, to the beach, the ocean, the earth. I saw myself, too, as an affront to nature. I wasn't sure how I'd become an affront to nature, but I had an idea that liquor was involved. I remember this night in a documentary way, as if it occurred in black-and-white. The dark water, sand, and footprints; the knowledge that this would be the last night I'd drink. I had little to go on—I guess it's always that way when you quit—other than the fact that I'd started swimming laps back home. The word *health* had a distant ring, and though I didn't know what it was or how to get it, though I didn't think I could find it on foot, I did believe that I might be able to swim to it.

So when we went back to Birmingham the next day, I didn't drink. Dennis quit four days later. The first Friday night was hard, but we had each other. We talked about the not drinking, how outrageous and audacious and hard it was. We liked Saturday mornings, though. They reminded us of childhood, the Gypsy thrill of a September morning. I swam my laps, and though my lungs were weak from congenital asthma and years of marijuana, my body made a path in the water. Six weeks passed, and in October we went back to the Gulf and swam in the ocean. I wore my goggles and studied the seaweed, coral, and fish, suddenly interested in things other than lust.

Dennis and I swam side by side. I didn't know then that the seaweed I was seeing for the first time is used for medicine and fertilizer, soup, jelly, even ice cream. I didn't know how to distinguish one shellfish from another. I'd never stopped to think about the continental shelf or how we swim on the ceiling of the sea. I didn't know about the oceanic under-world—the currents that flow like rivers, trenches as deep as the Grand Canyon, mountains with peaks high as the Himalayas. I wasn't aware that the sand had arrived as sediment carried by the Mississippi from the watersheds of the Ohio and Missouri, dropped by a master stream at the Delta, then reworked by currents that brought it here to the Florida panhandle, where I'd come every summer of my life. I didn't know that some sand grains were from igneous rocks of the Appalachians that had—like my family—migrated to lower places. I didn't know that sand grains are travelers. I didn't know that what I was seeing was more than a single thing, that sand is a mix of translucent grains of quartz and dull feldspar with flakes of mica. In short, I didn't know anything.

I didn't know anything because I had never stopped running from myself long enough "To see a World in a Grain of Sand,/and a Heaven in a Wild Flower,/Hold Infinity in the palm of your hand,/and Eternity in an hour," as William Blake had told us to do. My mother had repeated this poem to me many times when I was a child, but I didn't get it. Maybe I did get it, but panic and lust had driven me away from the singularity of a moment in time. But that afternoon in October 1983, I felt the sun on my back, and I sometimes glanced underwater to see Dennis's lean body. He'd come from living water, as I had—as we all do. The womb and the sea both pulse with life-giving minerals. The Chinese character for the word *sea* combines the characters of water, plant, and mother. But when we are born, we forget.

The water remembers us, though.

And that day, the long-shore current took us westward. We didn't know what it was doing for us. We felt like we were swimming against something or, at best, running in place. Or maybe we weren't even aware of the passage of time and space, because we were looking at the fish and shells. We embraced underwater, wrapping our bodies so that our legs and arms—all eight of them—made us into a single octopus, one of the most intelligent and peaceful animals of the sea, capable of being hurt, like us.

In time, we disentangled and swam as separate mammals, more alive than we'd ever been, with a morsel of hope that we might be able to live without liquor. We left the sandbar and swam back through the deeper water, until the light waves took us closer and closer to shore. I didn't want to stand up. I was afraid to rely on the upright position. I'm not meant to walk erect, on land, I thought, as I let the sandy ocean floor scrape my belly and the shells rub my thighs raw. I stayed suspended as long as I could, but finally I was washed completely ashore, and so was Dennis. We rolled over, sat up, and tried to get our bearings. The long-shore current had taken us so far! We were way downshore from where we'd started. We'd done so little and been helped so much.

But then, back in Birmingham, toward the end of October, I went to see Nick. I did it on impulse as a substitute for the drink I wanted. *One last time.*

And I got pregnant.

My gynecologist was the fertility specialist I'd been seeing for four years. He was confused and hurt that I was in this situation, but he tried to be clinical. "If conception occurred with the other man," he said, "it could be that you're just not able to conceive with your husband. Sometimes this happens," he went on, tapping a pen against my chart. "Sometimes a particular set of egg and sperm just won't unite," he told me.

His office was dark—no window. I begged him to tell me there was a paternity test that could be performed on the six-week-old baby in my uterus.

"There's just not," he replied.

"Can't you tell whose it is?" I persisted.

"No," he said, peering at me over his half-rim glasses.

I brought out my temperature chart, and he looked at me incredulously. He couldn't believe I'd kept up with it through an affair. I couldn't believe I'd kept it, either. The ovulation peak was on the fourteenth day. I'd been with Nick on the eleventh day of the cycle, Dennis on the seventeenth.

He studied it, moving it under his Tiffany lamp as if to get an angle that might shed light on the dilemma. After a while, he turned his palms up. "I'm sorry," he told me. "I've never been in this situation with a patient."

Sometimes when I start to feel ashamed, I turn to ice. I become cold-blooded, like a reptile.

"I can't have this baby," I told him evenly. "I don't know whose it is."

"Then I can refer you to somebody here who will do it," he told me. I understood that he couldn't say the word. He was, after all, a fertility doctor.

"Can't *you* just do a D&C?" I asked.

"No," he replied.

I sat in a chair, his big desk an insurmountable barrier.

"Then refer me," I relented.

I went back to work—work being counseling drug addicts at a methadone clinic in a yellow brick building that was once a funeral home. I parked in the gravel, where we all parked, and I went inside. It was Friday. I called the doctor's office to get an appointment time for the procedure on Monday. Then I went home.

It's amazing how simple the blueprint is, how quickly we develop an X-ray of a person's personality, how we can't hide our pranks and quirks and sins from the other, and because we can't hide, we become—in marriage—a hiding place for one another.

We'd been together for eight years by the time I drove home from work to tell Dennis that I had scheduled the abortion. We had a wrenching weekend, with periods of silence and utter failure to communicate what this all meant—for the future, for our marriage. I knew he hadn't wanted Claire Miller, his college girlfriend, to abort. He'd wanted to marry her and have that baby. I didn't know if he wanted this baby or not. I never asked him. I just knew I was not going to have it, because I didn't know who it belonged to. It never crossed my mind that it didn't belong to any of us.

The next Monday I walked into the medical center, finally on the OB side of the clinic with all the poor mothers, but it wasn't to have a baby. I told the receptionist that I was there for an abortion. She said, "I will need the $150 in cash," and I took it from my wallet, where I'd stuffed the bills next to the photo ID that allowed me to interview inmates at the county jail when I was at work.

"I work for the university," I told her. "Department of Psychiatry, Substance Abuse. Treatment Alternatives to Street Crime," I said, as if this might make my presence here easier for both of us.

"You can fill out this form and then wait until your name is called," she told me, and put my money in a drawer. After a few minutes I was called in to see a social worker. This was particularly humiliating. I gave her my story.

"Sometimes you have to go through things to get your priorities straight," she said. I knew she was glad she wasn't on my side of the desk.

I went into the room and a nurse took my vital signs. I told her that I'd had an ectopic pregnancy in the past and asked, "What if this one is in the other tube?"

The nurse's chin was up.

"He'll know if he gets it," she told me, and nodded to the suction machine. She saw that I saw what would be used, and she explained that it was a vacuum curettage unit. In the lower compartment was the suction pump and the motor. The large bottle, she said, was where the *products of conception* were collected, and the second bottle served as an overflow compartment that prevented aspirated fluid and blood from reaching the vacuum source.

I put my feet in the stirrups, which had been lined with lamb's wool for soft padding and warmth. The doctor came in and stood near my head. It was the first time I'd met him, and I saw that he was a kind and decent man who would neither make light of nor dramatize the situation. He was here, performing this procedure, as part of his profession. I was, and will always be, grateful for his quiet dignity. The nurses' faces were drawn, and nobody wanted to make eye contact. We were all in this together. My heart was pounding. I picked a spot on the wall, just like a dancer. The doctor prepared to turn on the machine. There was a knock at the door.

It was the social worker.

"Somebody's here to see you," she said.

Dennis came in.

He hadn't planned to be here, but I somehow knew he would be.

I felt the speculum being inserted, the cervix being grasped and gently pulled forward by the tenaculum.

"I'm stretching the opening to the uterus," Dr. Bromberg told me, "so that I can insert the cannula." Dennis took my hand. He was up by my head, where he would stand someday while I gave birth to grace itself. But at that moment, we were trying not to look as Dr. Bromberg attached the cannula to the vacuum aspirator. He told us that *vacuum, suction*, and *aspiration* were all terms used to describe the same technique. He said that negative pressure was created within the uterine cavity, which allowed cleavage of the *products of conception* along the decidua without disturbing the myometrium. I didn't ask what any of that meant. Negative pressure would be achieved by a surgical pump. The two large bottles were for the evacuated uterine contents and overflow. A gauge would protect the pressure level, he said. An adjustment control valve would assure the right degree of suction. He warned that I might feel the force of the suction at first, but that it would subside after my uterus adjusted to what was being asked of it. He also warned that the noise from the machine might resemble the suction accompanying a dental procedure, and that this would be caused by a piece of tissue briefly blocking the suction tube. But when the piece cleared, the products of conception would continue to flow through the tube into the bottle. The uterus would then empty rapidly, and though this might cause more cramping, it would indicate that we were successfully completing the procedure.

Dennis looked startled and hurt, like a lost boy—and I saw myself in his eyes. Then he bent down and put his face in my hair. We breathed in and out. I knew why the curette and tubing they inserted were transparent. It was so the amniotic fluid and *products of conception* would be visible to the doctor. I bore down in the way I'd someday obey the urge to push. But at that moment the contractions were forced on me, and what I remember most is the tugging, the pulling, the way flesh clung to flesh, the way it wouldn't let go. The suction was, of course, strong enough to pull the embryo from my womb. The cannula, curette, dilator, speculum, tenaculum worked perfectly. The baby we'd longed for was sucked away.

One afternoon in late March, I picked a few pansies in the yard—yellow and purple. I put them in a tiny oval vase and went inside. I intended to put them on the table, but I never made it to the table. I was by the stove when it happened. I set the vase on the stove, which was a putrid, kitchen-appliance green. I slid to the floor slowly, my hands moving over the silver oven handle past the glass door to the drawer below, which held pots and pans and bowls that had once belonged to my grandmothers and were now entrusted to me. The sky to the west threw back the light of sunset. I can't make this more or less than what it was. I was a woman on my knees in my kitchen. I knew I had done something unspeakable. But I also knew, in that moment, that I was not going to be punished for it. And even though two more cycles occurred before Ashley's conception, I was delivered that day in March. And no matter how bad a girl I was and still am, I was delivered that day in March. And no matter how insane life has become or will become, I was delivered that day in March. And no matter how we baby boomers insist on questioning spirituality to death, the truth is that Somebody paid the price for us.

Ashley was born in January 1985—in the seventeenth month of her mother's and father's sobriety. She was nine days late, but right on time. We could not have had her any sooner.

Dennis took her from my arms, and I watched him walk out of the delivery room with her, staring down at her big blue eyes. A year later, he wrote a story in which a father addresses his daughter:

It is not an exaggeration when I say that we loved you before you were born, before you were even conceived. This is just in the nature of longing, particularly when it's for something that you think you'll never have. We thought we'd never be able to have a child. We had been trying for almost ten years. And the passion your mother and I felt for one another was too strong and too dangerous for us to keep it between ourselves forever. Eventually, without you, it would have sent us spiralling away from one another. What I'm saying is that we needed you more than you ever needed us.

family

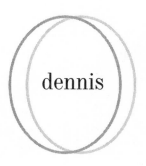

dennis

One night, a Sunday, I was grading papers late when I heard the sound of gunfire from somewhere in the neighborhood. I walked to the bedroom. Vicki stirred, but I don't think either she or Ashley woke up. I went out on the front steps and looked across Green Springs Avenue. There was a man running through the yards. He jumped into a waiting car— its engine was idling, although the headlights were out. The car took off at a leisurely pace. I ducked. After the car passed, I tried to get the license number, but couldn't. Then I waited, crouched behind the banister, breathing hard. There weren't any more shots.

I walked around the block. Nobody's lights were on. I was afraid I'd imagined the whole thing, but when I returned to the house, I called the police anyway. Except for mine, they hadn't gotten any reports of trouble, but they were going to check things out. Later I saw their patrol car meandering through the neighborhood, its searchlight touching every door along the length of Green Springs Avenue.

The next day I found out what had happened. Somebody had tried to steal a car from the carport belonging to our neighbors across the avenue, a retired couple I'll call the Finches. The Finches had opened fire from their bedroom window. Both of them had guns. For some reason, the thief had continued to try to hot-wire the car. That's why there were so many shots. None of the Finches' shots hit the thief, though. He must have been the guy I saw running down the avenue, a very lucky man.

The moment galvanized a feeling I'd been having of late. The city, particularly our neighborhood, was no place to raise a child. It was as dangerous in its way as El Salvador. And I think I may have employed that argument when I tried to talk Vicki into using her inheritance from Aunt Weeby as a down payment on some land in the woods. It's true I had a tendency toward the reclusive, trapped between the desire to be alone and the fear of being lonely. But I had always wanted to live in the woods for other reasons, too. My childhood had been spent drawing solace from nature. What I knew about the spiritual world, I knew from the way it manifested itself in the distant drone of cicadas and the texture of moss on a rock outcropping. I craved a patch of woods the way some men crave the illuminated playing field. It was the place, I thought, where I could most be myself.

To me, the house on Green Springs Avenue represented the life Vicki and I had left behind—the helter-skelter madness of booze and desire, not always for each other. I was about to turn forty, and I wanted to start over somewhere else, a nice little place in a valley where I could be, as William Carlos Williams puts it, "the happy genius of my household."

Two other factors also entered the equation. First, my father had emphysema; second, I was due to come up for tenure at the university. In short, I wanted to be closer to my father and as far away from the university as I could get.

When Vicki was pregnant with Laura, we made our annual trip to the Florida panhandle, where we stayed for a week at the condominium Vicki's parents owned. Vicki was having morning sickness, particularly at the sound of Billy Joel's "Uptown Girl." I was, in turn, moody and unsympathetic. I looked at Ashley, dreamy and sunburned, and Vicki, preoccupied with the drama of her pregnancy, and I understood that my life was closing in around me. The city was at fault, I reasoned.

A year later, we bought three acres of land in a wooded valley north of town, next to a larger tract that belonged to one of Vicki's uncles. We were ten minutes from my father's house, and in three directions from our property stretched the largest expanse of undeveloped land in the county— thousands of acres of hardwood forest, most owned by the Indian Valley Boy Scout Camp, a paper company, a group of investing doctors, and a local Italian family named the Tombrellos. We bought our three acres from two of the Tombrello brothers, who had split it off from their holdings as a personal favor to Vicki's uncle. Before we closed on the deal, the Tombrello brothers called with a final question. They wanted to make sure that Vicki and her uncle were blood kin.

Vicki was less enthusiastic than I was about building a house in the woods, but we found some plans we both liked in the local Sunday paper, and one of my father's church friends, a contractor, agreed to build the house for us at a very fair price. I drove Dad to the property one afternoon and showed him the spot where our house would sit, perched on a hill of oak and hickory above a small lake backed by limestone cliffs.

Dad didn't get out of the car. He was too sick by then. But later he pored over the house plans with me at his kitchen table, the green oxygen tank at his side. He studied the room dimensions, the open arrangement of the great room and kitchen. He considered the bathrooms, the closets, and he imagined the view from the breakfast bay window. He thought this would be a very fine house, and he was proud of Vicki and me. He had always wanted to have a house built, but it was an extravagance my mother had never allowed. When I went off to college, and she and Dad sold the white frame bungalow on Eightieth Street, they moved into a tiny two-bedroom brick home just inside the city limits.

Dad had to be satisfied with building a storage shed in his back yard, one side for his tools, the other for what he envisioned would be my mother's art studio. Dad and two of his brothers did the framing, plywood sheathing, and roof. A friend had helped with the foundation and electrical work. The shed was an impressive green structure from a design in *Popular Science*, with skylights made of plexiglass, glass itself being too dear. I think the building of that structure was one of the happiest times of my father's life. He had worked in an office for thirty years, pushing a pencil, as he put it. This was something different and invigorating, an escape from the tiny brick house that my mother always kept at eighty degrees to avoid the expense of air conditioning.

When he wasn't at work in the storage shed, Dad enjoyed just walking into the back yard and looking at what he'd accomplished with his hands. Inside, his tools lay well oiled and perfectly ordered—the hammers, wrenches, and screwdrivers mounted on the wall in brackets according to size, the orange extension cords coiled and ready, the blade of the table saw gleaming in the light from the plexiglass overhead. Dad did household repairs in this shed and made the frames for mother's paintings, which they carried in his orange Astre station wagon to malls and sidewalk art shows. Mother's paintings were good, and she always underpriced her competitors. Sometimes she gave paintings to family members and friends, but she had the disconcerting habit of taking them back, right off the walls, when she needed them for her next show. As I recall, she never painted in her side of the backyard house Dad built, but she did store some of her materials there.

For these or maybe other reasons, my father took more than usual interest in the house Vicki and I were building. Every day I touched base with him to let him know how the construction was going—the land being cleared, the footings being poured, the laying of the basement slab, the block foundation rising, the framing, the roofing, the insulation, electrical wiring, and plumbing, the Sheetrock and mudding. I told him about the installation of the septic system and about our plans to get the well driller out. Dad nodded. He asked a lot of questions. But he never saw any of the work in progress. And he never saw the completed house.

My father died on the day the well came in.

That afternoon, when I visited the site, the well driller told me he had hit water at 250 feet. He asked me to put my ear to the hole so I could hear the water running out of a distant rock face and into a pool at the bottom of the well.

"The good news is that you've got water," the well driller said. "The bad news is that it's contained in a chamber in the rock. We can hear where the water's coming into the chamber, but we don't know where it's going out."

"I don't understand what you mean," I said.

"Imagine a chamber of the heart," the well driller said. He molded his hands into the shape of a heart and alternately squeezed and released. "There's blood coming in. There's blood going out," he said. "This well's like that. We can hear the water coming in, but we also know it must be going out. What we don't know is how much water the chamber holds at any given moment. But I've pumped it and pumped it, and it has recovered every time. I can show you the numbers." And he did, squinting into the glare of sunlight on his crumpled, muddy sheet. "This well's not producing as much water as I'd like," he said, "but I believe there's sufficient water here to meet all your foreseeable needs."

I looked at him hard. This well driller had a red beard and a doctorate in philosophy. He had taken up well digging late in life, out of disillusionment, I supposed, with the university. He knew that my father had died that morning. I wondered if that was why he had used the metaphor of the human heart. But he didn't say anything more about chambers of either rock or flesh. He simply went about his business. He installed a submersible pump, capped and sealed the well, and ran pipe from it to the diaphragm tank in our basement. He also ran electrical wire from the pump to the fuse box. When he flipped the switch, the pump came on soundlessly. We turned on every faucet in the house—in the girls' bathroom, in our whirlpool tub, in the dishwasher and washing machine and kitchen sink. The pipes sang. We had water, plenty of it, and though it was muddy and filled with tiny gray pebbles, cuttings from the limestone bedrock he'd drilled into, the well driller assured us the water would clear. Later, he sent us a bill for $5,000. It seemed like a fortune, but not entirely unreasonable, we thought, for all the water we would ever need.

We moved into our new house on July 3, 1988. It was in the middle of the longest drought in the history of the state. That afternoon I went into the woods and found a dogwood tree, one my neighbors said was far too large to be transplanted. I dug it up anyway—despite its size, despite the season, despite the drought—and brought it to a prominent spot beside our house, where Vicki and I and our daughters planted it in memory of my father. We watered the tree with water from the well that had come in on the day he died.

One month later, the well went dry.

We shut off the pump and gave the well a rest. After several days, we tried again. The well dribbled, belched mud, and gave up the ghost. And we found ourselves in the middle of a true water crisis. We hooked dozens of garden hoses from our house to our nearest neighbor's well. Since our nearest neighbor was Vicki's uncle, this posed no problem, except that the garden hoses sprang leaks and had to be replaced on a continuous basis. And the water pressure was too low for any but the simplest of household needs. We couldn't water our shrubs or grass. They, like even the oaks in the valley, were starting to die in the merciless heat.

But I decided I wouldn't let my father's dogwood tree die. Every morning and afternoon I brought water uphill by hand in buckets from the lake. And when we finally had a pipe run underground from our neighbor's well to ours, I continued to water the dogwood twice a day, morning and evening, until early September, when the drought finally ended and the rains came, like grace itself.

My time in the wooded valley was both the darkest and the happiest of my adult life. Sometimes I would get up before dawn, even in winter, and hike to a place where the creek emptied into a deep pool. There I would take off my clothes, wade in, and watch morning come. The sun would hit the feathery tops of the pines and then work its way slowly down. The crows would caw high on the ridge. And sometimes a pair of wood ducks would fly directly over my head, their eyes steady and their wings beating like the sound of my own heart.

I didn't mind the drive into the city so much after that. No matter what happened that day at the university, I knew I would be coming home to the healing of the woods. I did not find my father there, although I hiked many miles looking for some sign of him. And the God of my childhood . . . well, I learned that that God was infinite in His subtlety as well. There would be no pronouncements for me in the woods, only the sound of wind through trees and the sight of the first green leaves emerging from the ginger and bloodroot.

I knew at the time that Vicki was unhappy in the valley. I attributed it to the exhaustion of caring for young children and the pressures of our precarious financial situation. When I finally suggested that her unease was a sign of a larger dissatisfaction with the marriage, she told me I was mistaken or reading too much into things.

Vicki didn't want to sit on the porch at night and listen to the bullfrogs at the base of the dam. It was difficult to coax her to hike to the abandoned Boy Scout camp at the end of the valley, although she took as much pleasure as I did in watching our daughters run down the trail toward the stand of poplars we called "the playground." It wasn't nature that repelled her—after all, she was the one who had shown me the ginger and bloodroot. What disturbed her, I think, was the finality of dark woods in a valley too steep to farm. Her longing for the outdoors was tied up with gardening, with flat, open land and deep, rich earth.

The dogwood tree we had planted in memory of my father was one of the things about the valley we all missed when we moved back into the city. After five years, we had decided to come back for the school system and the texture of a settled and child-filled neighborhood. It was hard for me and the girls, especially Laura, who had taken to the woods as her natural element. But it was the right thing to do, and I have never seriously regretted it. The things I regret the most in life have been entirely of my own making.

In order to sell our house in the valley, we had to have another well drilled there, at an additional cost of $5,000. This time we used a different well driller. The red-bearded philosopher had left the well business entirely, and our new man wasn't a philosopher. He was simply the only other well driller we could find.

This new well driller had a long list of customers ahead of us. He said he didn't think he could get to us in time to close on our house, but one day he showed up unexpectedly with his huge drilling rig. He said that God had told him to move our names to the top of his list. And he found water in an unconfined aquifer a few feet away from our old well, water that came so easily and with such force that it seemed to have no end. That was when I learned that even in the severest drought there is more water than we will ever need—directly beneath our feet.

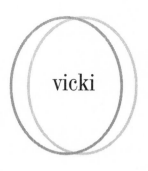

vicki

The five years we lived out in the woods were not good for me. In retrospect, I realize I didn't want to leave the city in the first place. Unlike Dennis, I had liked the house on Green Springs Avenue. I think I agreed to move because I saw a desperation in him that scared me. He *had* to flee. I knew, though, from the moment we moved, that I was going to be unhappy in the woods. I had quit my job as a social worker because I'd gotten a writing grant. But I missed my colleagues in a way I hadn't anticipated. I missed working. I found myself living like a hermit—no library nearby, no coffee shops or art museums or friends, only trees and a dry well. The cicadas and bullfrogs hurt my ears at night, the stars were too bright, and I was overwhelmed by the demands of motherhood. I felt asexual. Breast-feeding was deeply satisfying, but I thought of my body as a self-service gas station. I had my children, my *children*—my life's desire. But I found myself driving to Food World at night as if in search of something I'd lost. It was like, when I gave birth, I had left myself on the delivery table and a ghost of me had risen and moved on.

The Ghost was up long, hard hours with colic, fever, and ear infections. Sometime during those years Ashley had a seizure and turned blue as we rushed her to the ER. As it turned out, it was only due to the high fever that had accompanied a case of chicken pox. But it left me, the Ghost, ice-cold with terror. The Ghost was almost afraid to love Ashley or Laura. If there are two tragedies in life—getting what you want and not getting what you want—then maybe I was happier when I didn't have what I wanted. Hadn't Janis Joplin warned us that "freedom's just another word for nothing left to lose"?

Now I had much to lose.

The Ghost searched her daughters' eyes.

It was painful for me to watch Dennis water the dogwood tree. He had latched on to it like a life-support system. When a parent dies, I now know, you're ripe for imprinting. You are a gosling. You follow the first thing you see. For Dennis, it was that tree.

I knew, in the weeks to come, that I wasn't going to last in the woods. I couldn't turn forty as a hermit. I wanted to move back to the city, where we didn't have to worry about whether the tree would live or if the well might go dry. I wanted to relocate myself, to find the part of me I'd left on the delivery table. And I was certain that this could occur only if we moved back to the city.

After five years, we did.

We moved to the neighborhood where we live now. The girls were older and more independent. The Ghost vanished, and I somehow came back to life.

By this time, Dennis had been denied, then granted tenure. His book *Lizard* had been published and translated into several languages. He had written *Salvation on Sand Mountain*.

We had been going back to church for some time now, to the inner-city church in which I'd grown up. I'd wanted to hold his hand during services, to feel with him the fine line between sensuality and spirituality.

There was more. The ideas of a Baptist pastor named Paul Duke had had a radical impact on me. He believed that the family can be the most dangerous of human institutions if all its interests and loyalties are turned inward. It is instinctual to take care of your own, but it is not enough: A family feeding only on itself will eat itself alive.

"I am come to set a man at variance against his father, and the daughter against her mother, and the daughter-in-law against her mother-in-law." It's not the kind of thing you'd cross-stitch and put on a kitchen wall. But the message is clear: We are challenged to find larger loyalties. A family must turn outward, must give itself away, in order to find itself. It's not an easy thing to do. It's harder to hold hands when you're making a circle that faces outward. Your shoulders have to give more. Your arms are bent back. Your heart is exposed.

I began to work with a handful of kids in our church through a group called Children on Mission. We organized a children-ministering-to-children literacy program, where one day a week Ashley, Laura, and the other kids helped at-risk inner-city kids learn to like books. The family served on an AIDS care team. We led a mission trip to Belize, where we worked in the flood-damaged village of Douglas on the Mexican border, and at a church called Pan de Vida in the mestizo community of San Pablo near Orange Walk Town, a scary, gang-infested place once known as Rambo Town because of its violent drug trade.

I began to see us as *called*. It is hard to describe this phenomenon except to say that it's like falling in love. You follow after bliss as if you're following a scent. The New Testament refers to this as "walking in the spirit."

But Dennis was after something deeper. His experience in the snake-handling churches had caused a spiritual quickening in him that both thrilled and terrified me. He wanted to hold up his hands, to speak in tongues with the handlers. He wasn't interested in singing "Amazing Grace" at a Baptist church in Birmingham. I lived in fear that he'd stand up in the middle of a sermon one day and get pentecostal. He started preaching to friends, using the hillbilly inflections of the Holiness people to indicate that he might be mocking when he urged us all to "get things right with the Lord." I was almost irritated with him, because he'd always been so spiritually reticent. But I knew he meant it. He couldn't do religion the normal way, because he'd never done anything the normal way— which was the thing I both loved and hated in him.

One night, when we were at the beach, Dennis suggested that he and I pray out loud. It was very awkward for me. I prayed for Jim Neel, Dennis's best friend, who had recently lost his brother. It felt easier to pray for somebody else.

When we got back home, we kept up the praying out loud. We would sit on the sofa in the mornings with the light coming in, a southern exposure that warmed the room. We were reading the New Testament, and we took a chapter a day. We read out loud, and the words seemed illuminated to me. I felt I was entering a new level of spiritual understanding, with Dennis as my mentor—just as he'd been with writing. I learned the language of prayer from him, the way you don't plan the words, you just let them come, like writing. I was often amazed at what came forth when I didn't think, I who had always found it difficult to talk eloquently.

"It's the Holy Spirit," Dennis told me when we'd open our eyes after the praying. "Instructing you."

I'd blink, adjusting to the brightness of the room.

Prayer was, in fact, better than writing. It gave shape and form to life. It was as if we were embarking on a journey together that was better than any drink or drug or lover.

dennis

It's true that we were happily settled in a suburb with good neighborhood schools and well-lit softball fields. Our children seemed to be experiencing the childhoods we'd wanted for them, with freedom, privacy, security, and lots of pets. Our neighborhood, a cul-de-sac with seven families and sixteen children, was clearly a paradise, and Vicki and I were lucky enough to know it at the time. There were days when I would pull into our street and marvel that I was married to the woman I loved. I thought I would spend the rest of my life with her in that house on the cul-de-sac, and I hoped that when we died, Vicki and I would go simultaneously, taking our last breaths at exactly the same time.

But other days I felt cornered in our cul-de-sac, miserable in the conventionality of bay windows and fake widow's walks. I had always hated lawns—it's another reason I had wanted to move to the woods—and now ours was the largest on the block. The grass was always on the verge of dying.

My despair shouldn't have come as a surprise. I'd always

been subject to episodes of severe depression—a family thing, I supposed, the dark interior of the Covington psyche, the origin of, or perhaps the price my family had paid for our laconic take on life. I seemed never to be satisfied unless I was in the process of decomposing myself. During the worst times in the valley, after my father died and I was denied tenure at the university and our financial situation seemed beyond rescue, I thought about putting a gun to my head. I didn't own a gun, but I imagined I did. That was the extent of it, though. Just thoughts. But even after I came up again for tenure and won it, and my first book was accepted for publication, and we had crawled mostly out of debt, even then, when I'd drive into the cul-de-sac, an apparent paradigm of American domesticity, I'd have the urge to run.

What kept me sane, in retrospect, was the presence of the Holy Ghost.

We never talked much about the Holy Ghost in the Methodist church in which I grew up, or in Vicki's home church, Southside Baptist, where we'd started going to services after we sobered up. In these churches there had been a lot of emphasis placed on the first two manifestations of the Trinity—God the Father and Jesus, His Son. But this Holy Ghost business was a little spooky, and it was privately understood that too much talk about that particular aspect of divinity could get you into a heap of trouble. You might start believing that God was still burning away in his bush somewhere, that he was still healing the blind and casting out demons and multiplying the fish and loaves to feed the poor. You might start shouting in the middle of a worship service. You might start speaking in tongues. There were some, we knew, back in the woods of certain Alabama counties, who drank poison and danced with rattlesnakes in their arms. You might turn into one of them. And then what would happen to you and your children's braces and your sober, manicured neighborhood?

You might start not caring what people thought. You might just get drunk in the Spirit. I did. It was good while it lasted, a miracle of sorts. In the course of researching *Salvation on Sand Mountain*, a book about the snake handlers of southern Appalachia, I discovered that God was not a metaphor, some distant and abstract hope. He was a spirit, alive and so close to us we could sometimes feel His breath on our hands. We could smell His spiritual skin. We could hear His voice. And always, if we asked in Jesus' name and were of one accord, He would descend in power to comfort, encourage, and enliven us.

The rattlesnakes did wonders for my depression. And the spirit that enveloped me at the handlers' services didn't disappear when I left church. It clung to me on the long drive home to Birmingham and took up residence in our house and in our marriage. This was what our lives as believers had been missing, I think, a sense of extremity, an encounter with the absurd. For to the unbeliever, the Holy Ghost has just got to be the height of absurdity—glossolalia, strychnine drinking, fire bottles, copperheads, and worshippers falling on their backs and writhing as though tormented by steam from an unseen flame.

For Vicki and me, it was the ultimate trip. We dove headlong into the Word. We usually had our devotions in the mornings, after one of us had taken the girls to school. We'd alternate reading chapters of the Gospels or Paul's letters to the early Church, and then we'd pray aloud together, our voices rising and merging into something very much like a song. But sometimes we'd stay up late at night to read our Bibles in bed and pray until we were crying with joy. We'd be "way out in the Spirit," as my handler brethren called it, transported through time and space toward the center of creation and the children of God that we might yet become.

One time two of our friends from the snake-handling church, Charles and Aline McGlocklin, came to Birmingham and blessed our house. "Praise the Lord, Brother Dennis!" Charles shouted as he got out of the car. He was an enormous man with a voice to match, a latter-day locust eater, a wearer of skins.

I glanced at the other driveways to make sure the husbands had all gone to work. For the most part they were attorneys and stockbrokers, religious men all, but accustomed to more sedate manifestations of the Spirit. I didn't worry so much about their wives. Some of them were pretty far out there with us.

"Oh, dear God, descend on us now," Charles said when we'd linked hands in a circle in our living room. "Garnish and sweep this house of all demons and naysayers and afflicted spirits and send them howling out into the streets."

"Amen," said Aline, her flawless face upturned to the light.

"Occupy this place," Charles said, "every nook and cranny. Keep guard when this family sleeps."

Amen.

Charles stamped his feet, and the china in the cupboards rattled.

"Pour out a blessing too big for this family's hearts to hold! Make them a place in paradise!"

Praise God.

"Increase their income one hundredfold!"

I glanced up, not knowing you could ask for things like that in prayer. And Aline went into her dreamlike keening then, not so much a speaking in tongues as a drawn-out tremolo of ecstasy. "*Akii, akii, akii . . .*" she said, and it reminded me of the sound of killdeer in the valley.

"Bless them!" Charles said with another stamp of his feet.

Then he led us from room to room, each prayer becoming more fervent and deep. All four of us were praying out loud, our voices winding around one another like coils of the selfsame snake. I can only imagine what an outside observer would have thought. But for Vicki and me, it was a spiritual high so intense that by the time Charles and Aline had left, we remarked to each other that it felt as though our house had been elevated on stilts and the walls had blown away to let in a cascade of light and air.

These days and nights did not last forever, though. I don't think ecstasy is intended to. For one thing, I had to distance myself enough from the handlers to get the book written, and in the writing I came to understand I'd never take up rattlesnakes again. I had daughters, after all, and a vocation in the world; so I thought what lay ahead was a shift—away from an emphasis on the signs and gifts of the spirit toward what Paul called "the fruit." The fruit of the spirit, he said, consisted of those characteristics, or qualities, of the Christian life that had to be cultivated—temperance, compassion, longsuffering, love. Most often, they grew in secret, in acts of simple service. It was a conclusion most Christians didn't have to take up rattlesnakes to reach, but all my life I had gone at things backwards. The hardest part of Christianity was not the giving in, but the giving out.

Vicki and I struggled in prayer to find a calling. And then I ran across a book called *Shallow Wells*.

Shallow Wells was that rarest of texts, a brief, dry, technical treatise that somehow stirred the emotions and opened windows on the world. Written in the 1970s by a Dutch engineering firm called DHV, it was an account of the firm's attempt to bring clean water to villages in the East African country of Tanzania by using inexpensive drilling equipment that could be operated by hand.

Nothing is more difficult for a former liberal-arts major to accept than the notion that water doesn't originate from a kitchen tap. Oh, certainly there are lakes and rivers. But the ground? Come on. Well then, it must be like the footage at the beginning of *The Beverly Hillbillies*, only this time water instead of oil shooting a hundred feet into the air.

What I did not know about water was enormous. It consisted of both the simplest things and the most profound.

I did not know that water—the universal solvent—dissolves more substances than any other liquid. It has a higher heat capacity, too, so it's critical in maintaining uniform body temperature. It is the source of the earth's atmosphere. In fact, the evaporation of individual water molecules ultimately is the energy that drives tornadoes and hurricanes. But the water contained in the atmosphere also serves to protect us. By blocking the sun's most harmful rays, and redirecting its heat back toward earth, water vapor prevents large fluctuations in temperature. Water preceded us and sustains us. It is the reason we can live on earth. Water is not only present in the oceans, rivers, lakes, and clouds, it is always present, unseen, under our feet.

I did not know that 97 percent of all available fresh water on earth is underground. It is contained in nearly every square inch of earth. But water is able to be retrieved usefully only from layers of earth that it saturates. The top surface of this saturated zone is called the water table. Beneath it, water is found in aquifers, layers of rock or rocklike material that are capable of both storing and yielding up water. Sand and gravel make excellent aquifers. So do loose alluvial soils. But solid-looking rocks like limestone and sandstone also make fine aquifers. Even harder rocks, like granite or quartz, can store water if they have been sufficiently fractured or weathered.

By now, our lives had been sufficiently fractured and weathered, but still I did not know that brokenness was not enough. In order to be an aquifer, a layer of earth must be both porous and permeable. The pores, or spaces within the rock (or between the grains of sand or pieces of gravel), allow the aquifer to store water. Unweathered marble, for instance, has very few pores and so can't store water effectively. Gravel, on the other hand, has numerous spaces for water to fill. But porosity alone is not enough. The pores must also be connected. Clay, which has plenty of pores and stores enormous quantities of water, is not generally an aquifer, because its pores are not sufficiently connected to allow water to escape. Both characteristics are essential. Porosity accounts for an aquifer's ability to store water. Permeability accounts for its ability to yield its water up.

. . .

To be broken and yet to be joined in our broken places. This was what Vicki and I needed in order to hold living water and, more important, to yield it up. In a way, water—like the Spirit—makes its own hiding places. There is power and subtlety in this act. Frozen water can fracture the hardest of rocks. Thawing snow washes boulders from the tops of mountains into rushing streams, where it grinds them into smaller and smaller pieces, until it deposits the gravel and alluvial sediment in the meanders of riverbeds. These deposits make some of the best aquifers in the world. In them, water waits for millennia, eventually allowing itself to be found.

Drilling a well sounds like a static and strictly linear process. You drill until you reach water, right? But water in an aquifer is under constant pressure from the weight of the rock and water above it. And since water moves from areas of high pressure toward areas of low pressure, the job of the well driller is to decrease pressure on the aquifer. The well driller doesn't "reach" water in the strict sense of the word. He simply takes pressure off the water, allowing it to escape into wells, where it then rises to the level of the water table, to be retrieved by bucket or pump.

I did not know that the faster you pump, the steeper the water table slopes toward the well and the faster the water rushes in. So the more you pump, the more water the well will produce. Of course, there is always the danger of "mining" the water, of depleting it more rapidly than it can be replaced. This is particularly a problem in areas where population or irrigation demands have outstripped available local water resources. Water tables are dropping precipitously in some Western states, in southern Florida, and in the Middle East. But overpumping is an exceptional case. As long as the aquifer is being recharged adequately through rainfall, the supply of water in a given well is virtually endless. The global water supply, after all, has remained constant for the past 500 million years.

This is what I learned about water over the months that followed. I also learned that one person, armed with only a hand auger, a well point, and a sledgehammer, could literally drive a well into the earth until he hit water. Two to four people could go deeper, using an augering device turned in tandem. Vicki and I could do it. Our girls could do it. We could become a family of well drillers. And in the search for actual water in a place like El Salvador, where the leading killer of children was unclean drinking water, maybe we could find the spiritual water that Jesus had talked about to the woman at the well. "Whosoever drinketh of this water shall thirst again; but whosoever drinketh of the water that I shall give him shall never thirst."

This was our prayer.

vicki

What we got, in reply, was my mother's diagnosis of Alzheimer's.

I'd known for a while that something bad was happening to her. An articulate woman, she was now stumbling in mid-sentence, like somebody learning a foreign language, unable to find a word she wanted. Her hands wouldn't do what her brain told them to do; simple things: peeling potatoes, buttoning buttons. By the time of her diagnosis, my father was already well advanced into Parkinson's disease. I was overwhelmed by the enormity of trying to care for them both.

When I was a little girl I had three recurring nightmares. In the first one, my mother had a twin who was mean and sinister. The scary part was that I didn't know who was the real mother and who was the impostor. In the second nightmare, I was behind the wheel of a car going sixty miles an hour. But I'm only a kid! How do I drive? The third: I'm running from a pack of wolves to my father's arms, but he keeps backing up and I know I'll never reach him in time.

I suddenly found myself, at midlife, living out all three childhood nightmares. Alzheimer's was robbing my mother of her sweet self, and I never knew whether the mean impostor was going to be there when I walked in the door. I was going sixty miles an hour, running two households, all the while wanting to scream, "I'm only a kid!" The pack of wolves was upon me, and my father's arms shook with Parkinson's.

I was ripe for an anchor when I met Kira's husband.

He was an ordinary man. I was interested in what he did for a living, which had nothing to do with the arts. He didn't have a bohemian bone in his body. He wore cuff links. He was only eight years older than me, but it was enough.

He had been pursuing me for a while, maybe even a couple of years, in the subtle and safe dance of midlife adults—eye contact that lasts just a fraction of a second longer than it should, but could still pass for normal, depending. Since he lived in the same community, I'd run in to him often. He was smooth, never insistent, but I knew he wanted something from me. I finally met him for lunch, then another time for coffee, and then we started meeting once a week, then twice a week. I felt guilty, but somehow entitled. After all, I was taking care of both my parents, running a household, being a mother, and writing a column for the newspaper. Didn't I deserve something *all my own*?

I'd generally hook up with him right after seeing my parents. I met him in parking lots mostly. I'd get in his car. Sometimes he'd have starched white shirts from the cleaner's hanging in the back seat, and they mesmerized me. I didn't know a man other than my dad who wore things like this.

144

He seemed to be made of steel. He'd often say, "You're in there," and tap his fingers against his sternum. But I didn't believe him, even though there was no reason not to, other than the fact that he reminded me of my father.

I wanted to dismantle him, to make him stop saying, "I'm busy today." I wanted to control him and at the same time lean on him. It was a primal, hurtful longing.

I wanted to be his daughter.

I spun quickly out of control. My old obsessive-compulsive ways set in. I dialed his work number a hundred times a day. Seeing him was like drinking. It made the world go away. I didn't care what kind of chance I was taking. He was controlled and stingy with his time and love, but that only made him more paternal in my eyes.

In retrospect, I think I was way more than he had bargained for. But I was in the midst of a psychodrama, and he was a central player. My mother had given up driving after she hit the downspout in her driveway. I started doing all their driving. I took Mother to get her hair fixed. I bought their groceries and their gas. Took Daddy to the chiropractor. Took him home. One Sunday, Mother spilled Communion juice all over her hands, and I searched her eyes for what this meant.

I wanted to be with her because she was the love of my life. But my dad was groping for my time, too. The distant, busy man suddenly *needed* me. He wanted to hold my hand crossing the street. Later, on the way to see Kira's husband, I'd listen to Rimsky-Korsakov's *Scheherazade*, based on the story of the captive woman who saves her life by telling stories to her captor. When I got to his car, I'd reach for his reticent hand. Oh, the power of a father's love withheld. The ache of it, the yearning for it. Kneeling for it, to it. Bending for it, arching up to it, coming to it. I'm your daughter, I'm your daughter, I'm your daughter, I say to it—a mantra.

Dennis had, by this time, met Chance. But I didn't know about her yet. In the summer of 1996, after I'd been seeing Kira's husband for two months or so, Dennis and I went to New York for his editor's wedding. We stayed in the city for a night and took the girls to see a show. I remember riding the hotel elevator up—it was a glass bubble. I looked at Dennis, aching with guilt that I hadn't told him yet. We'd always told each other everything, eventually. I remember staring at him in the elevator, terrified by the impending calamity, but thinking, Your love can save me.

The next morning we took the train up the Hudson to Poughkeepsie, rented a car, and drove to Rhinebeck, where the wedding was to be. We stayed at a bed-and-breakfast that was billed as a ranch. Every room had a Western motif. There was the Arizona Room, the Wyoming Room, and the Montana Room. A few horses dotted the landscape, but you couldn't ride them. You could just stare at them over the fence and wish.

We slept under an overturned canoe suspended from the ceiling. On the wall was a saddle, an Indian headdress, and a rug. We got up the day of the wedding and stared at the horses while we ate doughnuts.

The wedding was held at an old German church. Dennis read the thirteenth chapter of I Corinthians—the one that talks about how love is patient and kind and keeps no score

146

of wrongs. The priest did a homily based on W. H. Auden's "Tell Me the Truth about Love."

The quality of light in upstate New York is worth noting.

It swept over the bride's blond hair—she was German and had a purity to her. It got into the eyes of the groom, and it made him look boyish.

I watched them, thinking to myself, There is no way to make you understand how innocent this moment is. There is no way to tell you what lies ahead for you. There is no way to tell you how you'll suffer, how you'll hurt each other in unspeakable ways.

That night, in the ranch house where we were staying, in the Wyoming Room, in the same room with the children, Dennis and I lay in bed and didn't talk. Something was at hand. I knew what we were about to do, and so did he.

We were under a big quilt.

"Who is it?" I asked him.

"Who is it with you?" he asked me. We were on our backs, looking up at the stucco ceiling. We weren't angry about what we were going to say; we just didn't know how to say it.

That's when we devised the finger game, whereby we asked each other a question, then held up one finger for "yes" and two for "no," with our eyes closed. I think the point was that neither of us would give up anything without the other doing so simultaneously. The first questions were broad and innocuous. Then we closed in, and finally, the names.

The night was over. The wedding was over. We'd danced under a canopy in Rhinebeck. It was the first time the children had ever seen us dance. They'd watched slantingly, as if

we were shunning them in a way they themselves didn't understand.

The bride and groom had led off and we'd all danced.
We'd danced fast and slow, in twos and in groups, and we'd
switched partners and danced some more. Sunset colored the
sky, and we kept dancing. The stars and the moon came out,
and we kept dancing. The bride and groom didn't want it to
end, and who could blame them? Who wants to go on with
life? Who wants to get in a car and drive back to the ranch
and get in a bed under a canoe in the Wyoming Room? Who
wants to arrive at the place where you can see the truth with
your eyes closed, where you know before you look that
you're both holding up the one finger and that the finger
says *yes*.

salvador

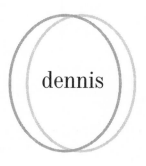

dennis

Our marriage had been through hard times all right, but that summer was the hardest of all. Technically, we were still sober and "working out our own soul's salvation in fear and trembling," as Paul put it. But we were also persisting in what we knew to be sin. There was no way to rationalize what we were doing to each other and to our children and to Chance and Kira's husband, the people we claimed to love.

Sometimes the well ministry seemed like a bad joke. Sure, we'd drill a well in El Salvador, if we just stayed together that long. And the spiritual distinctions we were trying to make didn't hold. "I'm not going to preach," I would say. "I'm not fit for that. I'm just going to be working with my hands." As if hands could be clean when the heart was a black hole.

We continued to plan for the mission trip to El Salvador. But in doing so, we were coming close to the unpardonable sin of blaspheming the Spirit. "Yes, but Jesus *liked* to hang out with sinners," we'd say, and we'd smile our old, bitter, ironic smiles.

One July morning, while the girls were away, we had one of the worst fights of our marriage, and that's saying something, because our past had been filled with doozies. In the drinking days, we'd fought mostly about other men and women. We got loud and physical, and in Ohio the fights always ended the same. I would storm out of the house just before dawn, often in winter, often in my underwear, and shout, "I'm going to Pittsburgh!"

I had never been to Pittsburgh. It was a sore point with me, and it made me even madder that Vicki never seemed to want to go. I don't know what I expected we would find in Pittsburgh. It is enough to say that the peculiar urge has since left me, perhaps as a consequence of sobering up.

Our sober fights, on the other hand, at least until that summer, had tended to be quiet and about mundane subjects— who wasn't doing his or her share of the housework, who was spending whom into bankruptcy, and who was being too easy, or too hard, on the girls. But on this particular July night, it was as though we had reverted to our drinking bouts, except that Pittsburgh was much too far away to be a credible threat.

The fight was about Kira's husband and Chance, and when it had crescendoed enough for me to storm out of the house, I went to the nearest corner phone booth and called Chance. We met at a clothing store not far from her house, but since there were likely to be people in the store she knew, we just pretended to be shopping in adjacent departments, and when one of us found an amusing item, we'd hold it up as though it were perfect for the other.

So much of what we'd done with one another had been

this sort of private play. I'd be leaving town and suddenly see her face in the airport corridor, a smile beneath her sunglasses as she passed, her only way of telling me goodbye and wishing me a good trip. Or there would be a card in my box at school from someone who identified herself as a student I'd had many years before. Or a cryptic message on my answering machine, garbled Spanish or French, the wrong number, the wrong *profesor*. So sorry, she'd say.

It was an affair of wistful silences, words between lines, meanings that resided in the corner of a mouth. But when we were alone, as we rarely were, the pent-up energy turned tender instead of desperate. I don't believe the word is *reticent*, but I do believe Chance and I were *cautious* with one another. Chance feared that she was a refuge for me at a troubled time in my marriage. And I was afraid I was simply a catalyst for her transition into a different sort of life from the one she'd known as wife and mother. Both of us, I think, were wrong. I cannot speak for her, of course, but I felt I had found a part of me that had been lost.

Chance and I were children. She was a girl with skinned knees, and I was a boy who was too often alone. That had been our starting point, as it had been for Vicki and me—a simple recognition of kinship and need. I think the greatest toll that marriage takes, in spite of its legendary benefits, is the destruction of childhood illusions. Contemporary American marriage may not be arranged by prospective in-laws, but it is still an arrangement of sorts—an arrangement of appearances, a mode of presentation, a divvying-up of duties, an alliance of calendars, a trust that cannot be touched until all its interest is earned. What we lose in the process is our nakedness, the very frailty that drew us together, the reason for the refuge that our marriage was to become.

By the time Vicki and I met Kira's husband and Chance, we were in danger of becoming our personae—a writing couple with a thoroughly public profile. We gave readings together, conducted workshops together, did book signings together. We were dogged by interviewers preoccupied with the novelty of two writers living under the same roof. So we had manufactured pat answers on everything from our differing attitudes toward deadlines—Vicki always finished her manuscripts before they were due; I preferred the gun-at-the-head routine—to the wisdom of sending query letters to editors, to the role of women in the church.

Chance and I, on the other hand, did not exist except as reflections in each other's eyes. Nobody cared what we thought about anything, because nobody was supposed to know who we were. I can only guess what I must have seemed like to her—perhaps an older, befuddled suitor with a disregard for clothes? To me, she was boyish, inquisitive, and persistently ironic—dismissive about everything except her art, which she simply refused to discuss at all. The work was what it was, and I have watched her examine it in a gallery with the same mixture of surprise and suspicion that I might find on the face of a patron who had never even seen the piece before—skeptical, as though the work might change in the process of being viewed. What Chance and I seemed to have, and what Vicki and I were in danger of losing, was the sense of our relationship as an ongoing work of art.

That night in the clothing store, I was intent on testing

Chance's resolve. In the parking lot I begged her to tell me she loved me, something she'd never done. When she finally did, I returned to my fragile household with a weapon I knew I could never use.

Vicki and I spent the rest of the summer keeping the water project alive while trying to understand what was happening to us, why after all these years we suddenly needed someone more than each other. I found relief in PVC pipe, which I had collected in every conceivable diameter and length, just in case we needed it in El Salvador.

I also became obsessed with tripods. You see, in order to hand-drill deeply enough to find water in a place like El Salvador, you have to have a sturdy tripod and a hand winch. Otherwise, you'd have to disconnect every piece of drill stem as you raised it from the hole and reconnect every piece before you lowered it back in. And you'd have to muscle all this by hand.

The design of the tripod was a testament to my inattention in math and physics classes. At first I tried PVC pipe, but the result was a twenty-foot-high, remarkably unstable contraption that looked like a giant daddy longlegs.

My friend Wayne Cook, an engineer and pilot, devised a more elegant and professional unit, made of two-by-fours and C-clamps, easy to bolt together or unbolt and then transport. But I'd given Wayne the wrong weight requirements, and steel pipe would be easier to find in El Salvador than the appropriate grade of lumber.

Doug Skiles, a young civil engineer from our church, came

up with the tripod we ultimately used. It was made from excess lengths of the drill stem itself, threaded together in a crown at the top that seemed sturdy enough to resist any degree of pressure we might put on it. The three of us— Wayne and Doug and I—must have appeared to our neighbors to be fools, but we were happily engaged in mechanical dreams, building tripods in our front yards. I particularly liked the sight of my front porch, stacked high with PVC pipe, drill stem, pump heads, and the like, so that Vicki, when she came home from a rendezvous with Kira's husband, would understand that I, at least, had been doing the Lord's work.

Of course, when Vicki got home, I would call it a day, shower, brush my hair straight back over my balding crown, and try to find a way to see Chance. This, I believe, is called domestic ennui.

So I escaped to El Salvador in the fall of 1996, to find the church in the capital that I'd been told was interested in water projects, Iglesia Bautista Emmanuel. Even the cabdriver had a hard time finding it. It was in a neighborhood called San Jacinto, at the corner of avenues Cuba and México. From the outside, it looked more like a machine shop than a church. But the singing coming from inside was full-throated and alive, and the sanctuary itself was full of light.

The first person I met after the service was Carlos Avalos, a young folk singer who led the church's mission at a slum in the nearby town of San Martín.

"I believe that I know you," he said.

"It's possible." I explained that I had been a journalist during the war.

"I know I recognize you."

"Maybe, but I'm not here as a journalist this time. I'm here as a well driller," I told him. "I'm looking for living water."

Carlos let that sink in, then nodded enthusiastically and embraced me. "You'll find it drilling for physical water," he said.

"So you understand what I mean?" I asked.

"Yes, yes, of course," he said. "You're an angel sent by God."

This was not what I had in mind.

"Yes, you are," he said. "This is what God does."

Carlos introduced me to a number of men and women who worked in the church's rural ministries, and then to Miguel Tomás Castro, the pastor. Miguel took me to lunch with his family, to a *pupusería* at Los Planes de Renderos, high above the city. Afterward, we sat on a bench in Balboa Park and talked while two of his daughters played kickball with a friend.

Miguel finally said, "There comes a time when you have to go to Jerusalem. Jesus instructed us to go, but it's risky business."

He smiled at his daughters, and then looked down at his hands. He said he had lost his youngest brother during the war, and one day after church, in front of his oldest daughter, who was seven at the time, Miguel himself was kidnapped by armed men in a car with tinted windows and no plates. They took him to National Police headquarters, where he was beaten and tortured. "They put a plastic bag over my head," he said. "It had some kind of powder in it. It cut off my breath."

He looked up at me. "Sometimes God sends us to places

and we don't know what is going to happen there. We just know something is going to happen."

The next day a young church worker, César Humberto López, took me to a ravine beyond the railroad tracks at San Martín, a town on the Pan-American Highway just east of San Salvador. César was in his thirties, divorced, but with custody of his five-year-old girl. A fountain of optimism and reckless energy, César went to night school and did public relations for the church in San Salvador and lived with war-orphaned teenagers in the church's youth home. On this day, he was my guide to places that needed water. San Martín had clean water, but the people who lived in the ravine did not.

I remembered San Martín from the war. I'd interviewed a woman there who would watch the war on television and then, when the newscast was over, take a chair to her back yard and watch the war for real. "The colors are better out here," she explained. On the day of the interview, there had been a gun battle in her back yard; one of the guerrillas had escaped by hiding in her outhouse. As we talked, helicopter gunships were strafing Guazapa volcano, the arc of the tracers preceding the clatter of the rounds.

So I'd been to San Martín, but never to the part of it where César took me—to the other side of the railroad tracks, where families were living in cardboard huts perched at the edge of a ravine. Open sewers ran under the tracks and into the ravine, along with rivers of trash and debris. The people who lived in the ravine itself drank water from a foul, wet-weather spring at the bottom. The government wouldn't run a water line from San Martín to the ravine, because the families who lived there were displaced people, squatters from other parts of the country who had supported the guerrillas during the war.

"It's a political problem," César told me. I prayed this wouldn't be the place we'd have to drill a well.

After touring the ravine, César and I drove to Suchitoto, a provincial capital that had been the scene of some of the heaviest fighting of the war. The name Suchitoto carried particular resonance for me. It was on the road to this town that *Newsweek* photographer John Hoagland had been killed in crossfire in 1984. A week later, when I'd tried to get to Suchitoto with a vanload of fellow journalists, the road was mined. We had to turn back. I'd imagined it as a place surrounded by vultures, the buildings in rubble or spray-painted black. Now it was odd seeing it for real, a quiet lakeside village with a picturesque colonial church.

Between Suchitoto and Zacamil, César pointed out the bombed-out ruins of Aguacuayo, one of the guerrilla strongholds during the war. Then he stopped along the road to show me the entrances to underground tunnels and bunkers, where hundreds of combatants and civilians had survived artillery barrages and infantry sweeps.

Zacamil itself was a small farming village—cattle and corn—high above Suchitoto and the reservoir at El Paraíso. The water problem at Zacamil was acute. A United Nations project to pump water from a spring catchment basin had foundered because of high diesel costs and pump failure. Zacamil did not look like a promising place for a hand-drilled well, but I told César I'd be back in April with an engineer to check it out.

vicki

I was sitting in the study when Dennis called to tell me these things. I wrote the name Miguel Castro in my notebook. Beside it I wrote, *San Martín—The Ravine*. I kept thinking of children standing at the edge of the ravine, so close they could see the pit below. *Jump*, I'd say involuntarily to myself.

But I was having a hard time thinking about the water project. As Christmas approached, I grew more detached from the children, from Dennis, from everything but the opiate of Kira's husband. He was, in ways, like a good therapist—detached, providing only a playground or a blank screen against which I could act out everything I was feeling. I'd get mad at him in an adolescent way, testing the limits of his love, brooding if he slighted me in any way. And whenever I forced his hand, got him to put a card on the table—whenever I detected that he was losing control or sensed a melting or a weakness in him, it empowered me in an erotic way.

By this time, I had stopped praying. I didn't believe in God or anything else. The spirituality Dennis and I had discovered through praying together had evaporated. I didn't see any way out of anything—the relationship with Kira's husband, the imprisonment of my parents' diseases, my depression.

But Dennis was insistent that we stay on course with the idea of a summer mission trip to El Salvador. "The ravine," he kept saying, as if the word itself carried charm. In the ravine was a mission. We'd conduct a ministry for women and children there, and we'd drill a well at the school at Las Burras.

"Put a note in the church bulletin," he said. "Say: Anybody interested in going to El Salvador this summer should contact you and me."

I did what he said to do.

People from the church started responding. Most of the people in our church were liberal Christian baby boomers who, like us, were trying to find something, *anything*, to do with their hands. Anything to make religious and political rhetoric blossom.

On Christmas Eve, my mother circled the kitchen like a malfunctioning windup toy. Her hands frustrated her. She tried to fold napkins, over and over, obsessed with this repetitious, meaningless task. Dennis cut her a grapefruit that my uncle had sent from Florida, but she couldn't remember how to hold her spoon or pick up a sandwich. I'd always believed that losing one's memory meant losing the capacity to recollect. I didn't know it meant losing the memory of how to swallow or tie a shoe. I saw that the dishes in the cabinet were dirty. I realized that she had been loading and unloading the dishwasher without washing them.

My dad handed me a pair of tiny scissors.

"My toenails," he said.

His Parkinson's prevented him from leaning forward. I sat on the floor. I was afraid of his feet. They were dry, cracked, and old, and I'd never really seen them up close. I'd seldom been near him in any physical way. I had only one childhood memory of his being near me, and that was a Sunday morning when he lifted me to his lap to buckle my black patent-leather shoes. I remember the way my feet looked in his big hands. Now I watched my hands move to touch his feet. I put his right foot on the oval footrest. His nails were yellow, hard, clawlike. I clipped them bit by bit.

I kept asking, "Am I hurting you?"

Laura sat beside me with some Jergen's lotion in her hand. We didn't say a word. She ran her nimble fingers between his toes. I followed her lead. We massaged his feet. She kneaded his ankles. The veins were all colors, red, blue, ocher, lavender, a maze of circulation bringing life to his feet. The more Laura and I rubbed, the more his feet changed. They lost all trace of old age, growing moist, pliant, sturdy.

Then we did Mother's feet.

"It's horrible, losing your mind," she said suddenly. Laura, beside me, didn't flinch.

"This is not for me. I don't want to live without a mind!" she declared.

"Maybe you can will yourself to die," I told her.

"Yes, I'm working on that," she said furiously. "I'm working on that."

Daddy kept watching the football game on TV, but at some point he said, to no one in particular, "When you're our age, all you have left is your children."

He nodded toward my mom with disgust. It was clear he wasn't handling her Alzheimer's well. He accused her of not trying hard enough when she simply couldn't do things. I had always romanticized their marriage, and now here was the end of it—my mother's brain atrophying and my dad's body shaking. My universe was chaos. Nobody was in charge.

I quit eating. I'd never starved myself before. It was interesting. I'd think of carvings, of cutting away parts and layers of my body. I wanted control. Alzheimer's was evil. It was satanic. It was sandpaper in a baby's eyes. It had no God, no garden, no story. It was worse than cancer or trapped elevators or children who fall into dark wells. It was the final trick, the clincher, the last laugh. It was proof that God didn't exist. It made me want to starve.

I liked being hungry. I liked the way hunger crawled inside my belly like a fetus. I wanted to stop taking in water, too. I wanted to be a desert, dry and parched. Life was only a mirage anyway, a big lie. It dawned on me that my mother looked like a tumbleweed—blowing, gray, windswept, in a dusty place in a land we'd never been to. We were blowing, all of us, through this barren life: my mother, my dad, my brother, Dennis, the girls, Chance and her family, Kira's husband and his family. We were all in the desert with no water, just miles and miles of sand. We weren't expecting rain or mercy. On certain days, when I felt better, I'd think maybe we were camels and we had enough water in these humps of ours to last us. But most of the time we were just nomads, wandering in the sand, getting wind of things, or so I told Kira's husband in the languid letter that I wrote to him after Christmas Day. It was a long one, on yellow legal paper, and I remember the way it looked, sticking out among the others in Kira's hands, the night she arrived at my door in January.

When I returned from Kira's house that day in January, Dennis was wearing his brown leather jacket, which he often does indoors, as if at any moment he might be called to cover a story.

While we were eating lunch, Kira called and said she wanted any gifts that her husband had given to me—there were a few pieces of lingerie and some tapes he'd made of songs he liked. I was, by then, experiencing something similar to Stockholm Syndrome. She was my captor, and I wanted to please her.

"I can't bring them over right now. My brother's picking me up in a minute," I told her. Randy and I were scheduled to go to Montgomery for a read-through of our stage adaptation of *The Last Hotel for Women*, which the Alabama Shakespeare Festival Theatre was considering.

"I'll come to you," Kira said.

"I'll leave everything in the mailbox," I replied.

So I put a few items in a sack and took it to the mailbox. I kept the tapes. A few minutes later she arrived. I stood at the window, watching her.

Her chin was up. I knew she wasn't through with me.

Randy arrived to pick me up a few minutes later. He is a burly man, an extrovert, an actor. We're alike only in that we have green eyes.

He turned on the windshield wipers. The rain was coming in sheets.

We talked for a while about our parents, about nursing

homes and sitters and bills and meal plans, the burden we bore in common, the burden of watching the people who gave us life start to lose theirs. Finally, I could bear it no longer.

"Have you had affairs?" I asked him.

"Why, you having one?" If he still smoked, this would have been the moment he'd pull the Marlboros from his pocket. But he'd quit after bypass surgery a few years back.

I told him about Kira's husband. I told him about Kira finding the letters and about being grilled by her. I realized, during the telling, that I'd not confided anything to my brother in many years. I realized, too, that he knew me well and that nothing I was telling him surprised him. Then he told me a story about being asked to dress up as Benjamin Franklin for a party of some kind. He was paid $500 for his time.

"And you know," he said, running a hand through his curls, "twenty years ago I would have thought, Damn, I can't believe I'm earning this much money, and ten years ago I would have thought, Not bad for so little effort, but right now, at this point in my life, I'm thinking, That was just a little bit humiliating; I'm feeling just a little whorish. I'm telling you this"—he said, and I turned to face him; he had one hand on the steering wheel, the other gesturing to me—"I'm telling you this because I want you to know that I know what it feels like to be in a degrading situation."

It was such a nice, big-brother thing to say.

We rode on a while. I looked at the clean burgundy interior of the car and remembered that his car used to be a wreck, like mine.

"You've gotten so neat," I commented.

I got through that day and the next and the next. I didn't talk to Kira's husband for a while, but when I finally did, he told me that Kira had built a fire in their fireplace and burned all my books, and all of Dennis's books, too. She'd told him, "Vicki's nothing more than a whore, why can't you see that?" as she tore every page from every novel, one at a time, tossing each one into the flames.

This infuriated me, so I kept seeing him.

And then, in March, he called me one morning and said, "I'm not going to see you anymore as long as I'm married to Kira."

When I was a little girl, my daddy brought me chewing gum when he returned home from work in the late afternoon. He brought either Juicy Fruit, Spearmint, or Doublemint. Juicy Fruit, the yellow kind, was my favorite, and when he brought it I felt he must love me. Doublemint made me feel bad, because it was his favorite, not mine. And if he brought Spearmint, the white kind, I believed it meant he almost loved me.

Kira's husband often brought me gum, too, because he knew I liked to chew it when I wrote. He always gave me Spearmint, and I never told him he was unknowingly giving me the I-almost-love-you brand. When he told me, that morning in March, that he wasn't going to see me anymore, I made an appointment to see Bonnie, my doctor. She put me on Prozac.

Then I went to see Dale, my pastor at the time.

I sat in his office—not your typical pastor's office and not your typical pastor. He was a runner, an artist, a bad boy. He knew about Kira's husband already and the letters and all that.

"I'm not sure I can go on," I told him.

He told me a story. He told me that he'd recently run a marathon with a mutual friend from the church. During the course of the race somebody handed her an orange wedge, and as she accepted it, she stumbled and fell on her face, so hard her glasses shattered. Dale knelt and urged her to get up. She did get up, kept going, and he ran alongside her. Whenever she started crying, he made her keep going. "We'll go to the medic's tent when it's all over," he told her.

Dale's most recent work was propped against the wall. It was an oil—a body bending forward, the leg muscles in pursuit of something up ahead, something I understood. I told him I liked the painting. I thanked him for the story of the runner. I thanked him for being my buddy. But as I left, I turned back.

"I don't think I'll ever get to the medic's tent," I told him.

When I got home, I sat on the front porch with the girls. They talked about school and basketball and all the things spinning in their brains. I watched them wistfully, thinking how, when something bad is happening to your mother, you deny it. You don't see it until she can no longer hide it from you.

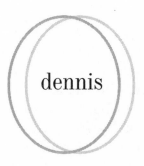

dennis

"What's wrong with Mom?" Laura asked me one spring night after Kira's husband had told Vicki he wouldn't be seeing her anymore.

"There's nothing wrong with her," I said. "It's just a rough time. She's under tremendous pressure because of what she's having to do for Gran and Granddaddy."

Laura looked directly at me. "That's what everybody always says," she said. "What's really wrong?"

How could I begin to draw for Laura the outline of what was "wrong" in the context of everything that had happened to Vicki and me during the previous year, to our marriage, our faith, our lives. It seemed as though the only connections that existed between us now were Laura herself and Ashley, and the idea of wells, this preposterous search for water in a tiny country a thousand miles away.

I wondered whether I had kept my parents together at a certain crucial stage, when my father was skating with a woman who worked at his office, and I was a babe in arms. Would my mother have started painting sooner if she hadn't had to care for an unexpected child? Would she have some-how gone back to school, assessed her life in ways other than tradition had dictated, set out on her own to experience the world? I think the answer to all of these questions is no. And that marks the difference between a generation born in 1912 and a generation born after 1947.

Even with children, Vicki and I didn't *have* to stay together. The culture had already swung to the idea of "blended fam-ilies." If a marriage went rotten, better for the kids to be out of it into something better than to stay and suffer the con-sequences.

But we were the Covingtons, "the mighty, mighty Cov-ingtons," we called ourselves. We buried animals together, went to Braves games, said grace, had fun, pure silly fun in ways my parents and I had seldom had. We liked each other's music. We allowed tasteless caricatures of other people. We invented other families, from Texas or Pakistan, and became them at the drop of a hat.

Sometimes I was Philip Shahid, a doctor who operated on beetles' noses, a very delicate enterprise, but one not much respected by my sister, Banana (or Ber*n*anner, as Laura called herself). Banana was from Leakey, Texas, by way of Alaska, and she had a dog that was, as Laura explained, "part Russian wolfhound and part Russian wolfhound."

Vicki, our Mrs. Shahid, was always noticing peculiar smells in the house. She had a million questions for Banana about this and other things, and Ashley, who had once made an excellent Polynesia to my Dr. Doolittle, would scream along with us in delight, until she decided the whole routine was beneath her dignity as a twelve-year-old.

Friday nights were our special times together. Sometimes

we'd listen to the Gospel Cavalcade on WDJC. The girls would do interpretive dance while Vicki and I amen'd. Or we'd tune, instead, to WRAX—the X—where Meredith Brooks would be howling out the "B" word. Nothing was sacred. We had no sense of taste.

Vicki and I did not have to stay together, but of course, in ways we did, or else we'd miss the happy madness that was our family's life. So I didn't answer Laura's question entirely truthfully. I pretended that nothing was wrong except ailing parents—Vicki's, not Laura's.

And in April I went back to El Salvador with Doug Skiles, the young civil engineer from our church in Birmingham. Doug and his wife, Laura, had gone with us to Belize the year before. At a marriage retreat later sponsored by our church—a onetime, serendipitous event—Vicki and I had mentioned the well idea. Doug later told me he'd felt a sensation like electricity running up his arm. When I asked him if he thought we could hand-drill such a well, he said, "I don't know, but whatever you do, count me in."

We took a lightweight augering set with us to Salvador, the one the girls and I had used to drill the well in our side yard. César, again, was our guide. At Zacamil, high in the mountains overlooking Suchitoto and the reservoir, Doug and I started drilling test holes, while a trio of curious Salvadorans and their cows looked on. The men ultimately took turns at the auger, too, but the going was rough. We kept running into rock and finally had to acknowledge that the geology of Zacamil wasn't right for hand-drilling, no matter how critical the village's need for clean water.

César retraced our steps toward the capital, stopping again

at San Martín. The prospect at the ravine, though, was even less hopeful than the one at Zacamil. Taking one look at the exposed basalt cliffs that plunged for hundreds of feet into the dry streambed below, Doug shook his head and said, "No use even getting the equipment out."

But instead of being discouraged that night, Doug and I were in a curiously euphoric state. On my previous trip to Iglesia Bautista Emmanuel, I'd met Rebecca Kragh, a medical doctor from Minnesota who was working in the eastern province of Usulután. She'd said the number one problem there was unclean water. Doug and I had taken out our geologic maps and discovered that the villages where Rebecca worked were on the fringes of a broad alluvial plain formed during eons of meandering by the Lempa River. The Lempa itself was filthy, a river of raw sewage from the capital, but its alluvial plain offered us the best hope yet of hand-drilling to clean water. The site was certainly worth a try. "If we can drill one well there, we can drill a hundred," Doug said. And as we talked deep into the night about water wells and drilling equipment, I thought about telling him everything, about Chance and Kira's husband, about the craziness Vicki and I were going through. But how could I have explained what an alluvial plain in El Salvador had to do with the desiccated state of my own marriage? And how could Doug, still in his twenties, newly married and expecting his first child, possibly understand?

The geologic maps were right. The next day, when Rebecca took Doug and me to the schoolyard at Las Burras, we sank a hole almost fifteen feet deep without encountering a single rock. That was as far as we could go with the lightweight augering set; we'd run out of extensions. But we knew, from the history of other wells in the area, that if we could just get down twelve feet more, we'd hit water. It would take heavier equipment and a tripod and more men, but we figured it was our best bet.

On our way back to the capital, Doug and I were talking about the logistics of getting a team of workers and all the necessary equipment out to the village, a good three-hour drive from the capital. Our Salvadoran hosts, meanwhile, were reminiscing about the recent National Assembly elections, in which the two major competing parties, arch enemies during the civil war, had fought peacefully at the ballot box to a virtual tie. The rightist party, called ARENA, had emerged with a single vote margin in the upcoming Assembly, 28 to 27, but the leftist FMLN, with whom our hosts clearly identified, had run an astonishingly close second. The FMLN was holding a victory dance of sorts that night in the capital, in front of the statue of El Salvador del Mundo. "You've got to come with us," César said. "It will be the party of the decade." And although Doug and I had sworn off any activity that might in the least be viewed as political, at that moment we were feeling buoyed enough by our success at Las Burras to consider the invitation seriously. A night on the town didn't sound like a bad idea at all.

Near San Vicente, in the shadow of the twin volcano known as Chinchóntepec, the traffic had slowed. There must have been an accident, I was thinking, and there had been. A small Toyota truck coming from the direction of San Salvador had run off the road and hit a tree. The truck had been transporting cows, one of which lay dead in the ditch on the left-hand side of the road. But the accident seemed oddly incidental. People were gathering on the right side of the highway, not the left. That's when I saw the dead man lying on the shoulder of the road, sprawled facedown in a puddle of blood. His car, a dark blue Toyota Celica, was undented. The man clearly had not been thrown from it. He lay exactly as he must have fallen, a substantial man in a dress shirt, vest, and neat green pants. His feet were splayed awkwardly in the gravel by the road. He had not been killed in an accident. He had been killed exactly where he stood.

Doug thought he saw a USAID decal on the side of the Celica, so we asked our host to make a U-turn and drive back. By this time, a police car had pulled up behind the body. Its headlights washed over the scene. If the dead man was an American official, I'd have to quit my resolve not to be a journalist on this trip. I got out my notebook, went straight to the policeman, and asked the question I'd asked a hundred times in El Salvador during the war: "*¿Que pasó aquí?*" What happened here?

The policeman glanced over my shoulder, toward the semicircle of people gathered at the foot of the body. "Ask her," he said. There was no doubt whom he meant, for the semicircle had formed like a backstop around an otherwise solitary figure, a young woman in a pale green dress, her empty hands held open in front of her, as though she were trying to hold on to an object no longer there.

"What happened, ma'am?" I asked.

"They killed him in front of my eyes," she said.

"Who?"

"The men in the truck. They'd run off the road and hit a

tree. We were on our way home from Apastepeque. My husband stopped to help. The men got out of the truck. They recognized him. One of them drew a gun. 'I'm going to kill you,' he said. He shot my husband three times in the chest." One of her hands went to her throat. "He vomited blood. And then he died."

Her name was Andrea Umana, and her husband, Carlos Zelaya Seeligman, had been the newly elected delegate to the Salvadoran National Assembly from San Vicente Province. He was a member of the ARENA party. That was the decal on the side of his car. He had been their one-vote majority in the Salvadoran National Assembly. Now he was dead.

Friends and relatives closed around the woman as the open-bed truck from the funeral home in San Vicente arrived. I had other questions, inappropriate questions. Had he been a good husband? Faithful, forgiving? Had she been a good wife? What was it like to know that they would never again have the luxury of simply riding in a car together, on a Sunday afternoon, talking about whatever it was they were talking about the moment before he pulled onto the shoulder of the road, got out of the car, and died?

I put away my notebook and headed back toward the church truck. "Political assassination," I said. "I don't know whether it was set up beforehand or whether it was just a spur-of-the-moment thing."

"That's the problem here," César said. "Since the war, everybody's got a gun. We're supposed to be at peace, but more people are being killed in political violence now than during the war."

A year later, César himself would be dead, shot five times

in the back as he was walking to church, a crime of passion, not politics, everyone would say.

But on that evening after the assassination of the ARENA party delegate, as we pulled back onto the Pan-American Highway into a dusk that had already settled for good, Doug whispered, "This is no place for our mission team."

"I know," I said.

We rode back to the capital in silence. And we didn't go to the dance, after all.

vicki

I didn't want to hear any of this. It reminded me too much of the stories Dennis told me when he was covering the war. I didn't want him to talk about it in front of the mission team that would be going to Salvador in June. But in late April, we called the team together for a meeting.

It's one thing to go out on a limb. It's another to take most of your friends with you. Before we got sober, Dennis and I used to have parties on Friday afternoons. He made margaritas. He was careful to make the salt rim razor-thin, but the idea was to get everybody real drunk, real quick. Putting friends in danger had been a real kicker for us. And I think this fact has always made me uncomfortable when we've led mission trips to foreign countries. I'm always aware that Dennis and I are "taking a buddy along for the ride," that we wield power over people if we choose to, that we want everybody to take a risk, and it's not always clear if the outcome will be destructive or redemptive.

We met in our living room. It wasn't a typical Baptist

mission team. It included a cocktail waitress, an editorial writer, a scientist who'd lost his wife to Lou Gehrig's disease, a drama teacher, a nephrologist and his daughter, a marathon runner, a seamstress, a financial consultant, a civil engineer, and a few children and college students. We were a mixture of baby boomers and Gen Xers, and most of us had been down some back roads.

The night of the team meeting, Dennis sat on the hearth. He told the group about the assassinated senator.

"Oh, so let's not go during dead-man-in-the-road season," Laura suggested.

Dennis went into the kitchen and returned to the living room, carrying the bayonet hand auger. It looked as light and insignificant as a majorette's baton.

"That's it?" Joey, the editorial writer, asked incredulously.

Dennis nodded. "This is it."

"It's state-of-the-art equipment," I said, wanting to convince the others we knew what we were doing and, at the same time, feeling like an absolute impostor.

"It does work," Ashley said. I looked at her strong, young arms, which had diligently worked the hand auger in the front yard, where we had gone down ten feet the Saturday before Easter and hit water.

Laura nodded in agreement.

I felt as if we were holding a Tupperware party or selling Amway, conspiring to convince others to join an enterprise. Dennis held the auger heads—the combination Edelman, which could be used in different soil types, and the Riverside bucket auger, both of which the kids had used in the yard. "This is amazing stuff," he said.

I watched everybody watch him. I knew they were thinking the same thing. They were thinking, This man is crazy,
but if he believes we're supposed to be well drillers, so be it.

Watching Dennis, I felt a familiar mixture of pride and fear.
It is hard for me to get interested in new information. My
mind is like granite. Dennis, on the other hand, is always
reeling in a new idea. This same group of friends had watched
him get dangerously close to his subjects while writing *Salvation on Sand Mountain*. They knew he'd picked up rattlesnakes in Holiness churches. They knew he was a Christian,
but also a journalist with a nose for trouble. I liked watching
the admiration on their faces. I saw him as I knew they were
seeing him—a rebel, a fool, a man like Jesus.

The Prozac I was taking to make me stop crying over my
mother's Alzheimer's and the abrupt goodbye to Kira's husband made my pupils dilate, and sometimes the light in a
room got cloudy, as if I'd just been to the ophthalmologist.
It was doing that now.

Toward the end of the meeting, we divvied up assign-
ments. Lia was to check with the public-health department
about the malaria pills and other inoculations. Clarice would
check on a smocking machine that didn't require electrical
power—in order to teach village women a lucrative art. Bob,
the scientist, would secure a water quality field kit. Doug was
to pressure-wash rust off some used drill rods we'd been storing in our basement and then oil up the couplings. Carl would
handle finances. Dennis would look for a place to practice
drilling a well here in Alabama, somewhere south of Montgomery, where the soil was more like that in El Salvador. In
the meantime, we'd all practice our Spanish.

178

At the end of the meeting, Dennis prayed. It was a prayer of humility. Nobody in this particular group had a smooth track record. And we knew that night, as we've always known, that we weren't going to Central America to save the Salvadorans. We were going to save ourselves.

The next Sunday, Dale preached a sermon on receiving grace. At the end of the service, Joey—the editorial writer—was coming up the pew with the offering plate when my mother stood up and started shouting, "Joey, Joey," and waving her hands madly. In retrospect, I believe she was trying to let somebody know that she didn't have her offering handy, but at the time it was a nightmare in the making. I grabbed her hand and led her toward the back door. I got her out into the vestibule, but she jerked away from me. I put my arms around her in a dead-lock embrace, and I led her outside. It was as if she were intoxicated—though she's never had a drink in her life—and for a moment I saw my old, drunk self in her eyes. "Mother," I pled. "It's me. It's Vicki."

Finally, she relented. She calmed to the point of whimpering. But I knew we'd passed some kind of marker. I'd read of the violent stage in Alzheimer's. The finality of the loss of her swept over me. All day I tried to invent distractions for myself. I baked. I shopped. I worked in the yard. I worked on the book. But the big distraction—Kira's husband—was no longer available. So I grieved for him and for my mother together, not even knowing the difference.

•   •   •

179

One night, about a week later, Laura and I were standing in the middle of the cul-de-sac, facing northwest. From where we were standing we could see Hale-Bopp just to the right of our house.

Laura was barefoot, in cutoff jeans—a replica of her rebel father. Only her unreasonable fears marked her as mine.

"Is a storm coming?" she asked, though the sky was clear.

"No," I told her.

We looked up at Hale-Bopp. The comet was dim, and I knew that we wouldn't see it after tonight, though it had lasted so much longer than anybody predicted.

Behind us, all the lights were on in our house. You could see inside the living room—my grandmother's table, Jim Neel's artwork, the loveseat and sofa where Dennis and I sat and prayed all those prayers.

"I can't believe we saw it over the Grand Canyon," Laura said of the comet. I looked over to the side yard, where we'd driven the practice well, where Laura often worked the pump, making the surface water that had collected in the casing spew forth.

A full moon had erupted.

"When will tornado season be over?" she asked. Her wispy blond hair was pulled back with a scrunchie.

"June," I told her.

"Has an F4 ever come through Birmingham?" she asked.

I told her I didn't know tornado classifications, and that I didn't know the tornadic history of Alabama either, aside from remembering the outbreaks in the summer of 1974 and the spring of 1977.

"What's wrong?" she asked me. I told her that Gran—my

mother—had had a bad day today, that she couldn't make her hands work right. Laura studied me to see if I was telling her the truth. Her eyes are a shade I can't define, a field that's constantly changing. Sometimes I try to dodge her eyes, because I'm afraid she's reading my mind.

"Why did God make storms?" she asked.

I shrugged.

"I mean, if he's so in control of the universe, why do I feel like a bug, a bug that he might simply stomp out with his big foot?" she asked.

I had no answer for her.

A week later, she turned ten. We celebrated her birthday by taking a few girls to a cabin in the woods, near a lake. Laura's friends were playing Truth or Dare. They inevitably chose Dare, and most of the dares involved stripping, splashing water, throwing food, or dismantling beds. They were making a big mess. Dennis and I sat on the porch staring at the water. The night was warm. A few night fishermen were casting nets, hoping for turtles or crawfish. I was reminding Dennis that when he used to write by hand, he'd do word counts of fifty, and he'd put tiny slash marks on the page.

"I did it, too," I said, edging closer to him. "I thought you were supposed to do it. I thought it was part of writing. I did it because you did it. I did everything you did."

He pulled me up to him, and I felt his rib cage under his T-shirt.

"You're such a good little sister," he said, a statement I found both gratifying and erotic. I draped a leg over his.

I was thinking of succulents. Since the trip to the desert, I'd been preoccupied with cacti. Cut it open, say the books, and inside is the vascular system whereby water is transported from the roots. The thick, waxy covering of the cactus protects it from water loss. Cacti can even draw water from fog, they can shed leaves on demand, and they will shrink inside the earth in order to survive. We sit there beside the lake, and I'm thinking of succulents. I wonder, I say to Dennis, which marriages are likely to survive when there's no water— the ones that are fused with passion or the ones that are based on friendship. We have roots of friendship *and* desire. We must have sucked up gallons and gallons of water, so that somewhere in the fiber of this marriage there is a vascular system capable of transporting water to the parched places, enabling us to survive with no rainfall for almost a year. I think these things under the stars, with my leg draped over his, watching the night fishermen's light on the water.

In mid-May, Doug Skiles arrived, hauling pieces of the equipment for the unit he was designing especially for the site in Usulután. He wasn't going to go on the big trip because his wife was pregnant. Doug is muscled and upbeat, and whenever he would leave our house, a part of him stayed in Dennis. At nightfall I looked out and saw Dennis, with his shirt off, still augering with the six-inch bit, widening the borehole by my garden.

I walked out to him.

"The soil in Salvador will be a lot easier than this," he said, knocking a wad of clay from the auger.

Things were falling into place, it seemed, until May 21— four months to the day since Kira had arrived waving the letters. I picked Ashley and Laura up at three o'clock and took them to the inner-city school where they worked in a children-ministering-to-children literacy program one day a week. Afterward, we went on to Wednesday-night prayer meeting. Dennis met us there, and I tried to chat with him as we ate chicken chow mein with rice. He didn't look at me or smile or show any sign of life.

"What's wrong?" I asked him.

He didn't say anything, but after dinner, as I was about to head up the stairs to a women's prayer group, he turned to see if anybody was in earshot.

He hesitated, and I knew bad news was coming.

"Kira mailed me copies of the letters you sent to her husband," he said.

"Did you read them?" I asked him.

"Yes."

I looked at the floor, at my tennis shoes and his. I didn't say anything, and I didn't know how I'd ever be able to say anything. We were in the basement of the church outside Fellowship Hall.

"I'm sorry," I told him. "I'm so sorry."

But it was as if the *sorry* had an echo, a reverberation that went all the way back to the beginning.

In bed that night he said, "It wasn't the things you'd think that hurt me. It was other things, things that might seem meaningless to an outside observer."

I knew what those things were. I knew it wasn't any words of longing or desire. I knew that I had, in one letter, said that one of his daughters "held her beauty at a distance." This was something that Dennis had once said to me, about me. And

I had also told Kira's husband how grateful I was to have been able to go through his father's death with him. There are things more intimate than sex.

Later that night, I was crying in bed, as I did every night during April—for my mother, for Kira's husband, for myself. Dennis handed me a copy of *Water Well Manual: A Practical Guide for Locating and Constructing Wells for Individual and Small Community Water Supplies*, as if he were handing me a prayer book or a self-help guide.

I opened the book, then let it fall on my chest. We lay in the semidarkness amid the stacks of engineering books and other debris on our bed.

I held Dennis's hand, and we watched the ceiling fan blades.

"I feel like I'm tripping," I told him.

"You are," he said.

Beside my bed was the notebook where I'd jotted down information about Dennis's trip to El Salvador in March— where he'd hooked up with Rebecca Kragh, the physician who'd told him about the clinic in Talpetades that needed a water well. There was a school in Las Burras, too, with no clean water. The children were drinking out of the Lempa River, and most of them had intestinal parasites.

Under my notebook was a copy of *Shallow Wells*, the book about the Sinyanga wells project in Tanzania. I'd tried to read it, but I couldn't get past the things I didn't understand. I couldn't see how a well was going to save a marriage, either. I did, however, love looking at the photographs of the light-weight equipment—the bits, bailer, handles, and extension rods, casing pipe, and clamps. These pieces they'd used in

Africa were the same pieces we'd used to drive the shallow well beside my garden. I pored over them, considering the possibilities of simplicity and connectedness, possibilities in which I still believed.

A neighbor's car pulled in, throwing light on the walls.

"Did you want to call Kira when you opened her letter?" I asked him.

The neighbor's car door opened. The dogs barked, and this caused a stir on the cul-de-sac. All the dogs barked, one by one, and then it was quiet.

"I thought about calling her," Dennis replied.

I could see his face in the dark, the jawline I know.

"I thought about calling to tell her I understood her need for revenge, and now she's done it, and it's over. Then I thought about telling her to go to hell. But I didn't call. I didn't do anything," he said.

The next day I stayed home from the writing loft, and so did Dennis. I put a bowl of raspberries on the table. The May sky was blue, and if you'd looked in on us, you might have thought, *Sublime.* I wanted to talk about the mess with Kira's husband, but I knew he didn't. I knew he couldn't, and it broke me up a few days later when a friend said she'd seen Dennis in the yard on Wednesday, the day he got the letters, kneeling by some white PVC pipe in the front yard, trying to assemble a homemade tripod for the lightweight well equipment.

"This is all that matters to me now," he'd told her, gesturing to the PVC pipe.

So I didn't press him about Kira and the letters. Instead, I asked him to tell me everything. I told him to speak slowly, to remember that my mind was made of granite. I told him to say it word by word, and he did. He told me that we start with a six-inch hand auger. We drill down until the walls start to collapse. When they do, we start casing it with steel pipe. Then we continue drilling with a four-inch hand auger, inside the casing. As we auger we simultaneously screw the casing down. When we hit the water table, we start bailing. We keep screwing the casing in until we get to a layer of clay, then we start augering again. Auger, bail, auger, bail, until we get to the level we want. When we reach that point, we put in the PVC filter pipe and plug it temporarily. We use gravel and sand from the Lempa River bank for the packing that goes between the filter pipe and the casing. Eventually, we pull the casing out.

The next day we drove to Lineville, Alabama, to a place called SIFAT, which is the acronym for Servants in Faith and Technology. Dennis had already been there once, and he'd come home euphoric, eager for me to see the operation. The place resembled a camp in some ways, with cabins, an office, and a mess hall.

People came there from all over the world to learn the use of appropriate technology in developing countries. SIFAT was a Christian organization, but there was no doctrinal creed other than the statement that the marginalizing of life, through preventable health crises, was "an affront to the Creator." In short, SIFAT seemed like a baby boomer's salvation.

We drove in and parked in the grass, near a cluster of daylilies. A dog ran up to meet us as if we were his family, home at last. I knelt to pet him, and for a brief instant felt that I had traveled back in time. I was at my grandmother's house, forty years ago. There was that feel to the place—rural, family, Southern.

Dennis took my hand and led me to an overturned bicycle that had been converted to a water-hauling device. As you turned the pedals with your hands, a cord brought water up by sheer surface tension. "Water has a natural tendency to hold on to things," Dennis reminded me. But still it looked like magic—the way that water was running up the rope.

We went to the nearest work shed, where an older man named Dale Fritz was working on a loom powered by a foot pedal.

"Hey," he said to Dennis, and reached under his worktable for a book. "I've been looking for you to come back. I have something for you."

He handed Dennis the book. Together they looked at a photograph of a boy in Indonesia who was "kicking in" a well by stomping on a piece of bamboo, forcing water down to find more water. He and Dennis chuckled over the utter simplicity of what the boy was doing, and I remembered for a moment the monster contraption that'd been used to drill that $5,000 well for us when we built our house in the woods.

Mr. Fritz gestured to me. "Is she your team?" he asked.

"Part of it," Dennis told him, and went on to say that the other nineteen members of the El Salvador team would be coming here in a few weeks to drill a practice well.

Mr. Fritz went back to his work. I studied his hands. They were big and worn, and they seemed to know what to do. They weren't a writer's hands.

"What would you call yourself?" I asked him.

"I'm an appropriate technologist," he replied.

Appropriate technology was a term I'd been hearing from Dennis. It involves the use of simple, inexpensive solutions to persistent world problems like hunger.

Later, when Dennis and I left the shed, he told me that Mr. Fritz had been a missionary to Afghanistan for thirteen years before coming to SIFAT to train workers. We walked past a clay oven and a solar water heater. In the distance was a garden where students had their hands in the dirt. As we got closer, I saw that the corn was ankle-high. The tomato plants had yellow flowers. I saw the beginnings of peas, squash, and peppers. Beside me was a bush with green, unripe fruit.

"Are these blueberries?" I called to the nearest student, who looked Latino.

He glanced up from the place where he knelt in the dirt. His chest was bare. He nodded *yes*, and then smiled at us, wiping his face with the back of his hand.

On the riverbank, Dennis lifted a piece of PVC pipe. "That's what we put in the well in the yard," I said.

"It's like putting your finger on the end of a drinking straw," Dennis told me as he pushed the pipe into the river. Pressure from the water it drew up would be enough to force a flapper valve to open, siphoning water from a river for irrigation.

We left the river and walked over to the cabin that held the SIFAT offices. I eyed the hand-printed cards that were a project of an ecumenical organization from India called SEEDS, formed to help deaf women who are outcasts in many a society learn the handicraft of painting pipal leaves to make greeting cards. On the wall was a cross-stitched message: GIVE ME A FISH AND I EAT FOR A DAY. TEACH ME TO FISH AND I EAT FOR A LIFETIME.

We got in the car and tried to find Third World Village, where children come to camp, sleep in hammocks, and learn the basics of appropriate technology. We couldn't find the village, though, so we just stopped the car in the middle of a field and ate the cream-cheese-and-olive sandwiches I'd packed. Afterward we climbed into a cow pasture, careful to avoid the bull. I like how cows gaze at humans as if we're only remotely interesting. I like how we stare back with grave intensity as if they know something we don't know, something we'd give anything to understand.

After a while we walked back to where we'd parked. Dennis put his fingers in the belt loops of my jeans and pushed me up against the car door. It was a familiar gesture. "I don't think we should do it here," I told him, and he smiled. We stood there for a long time, searching each other's eyes, like we knew something we couldn't say. I think that we knew, at that moment, that we were going to survive.

There was a point somewhere in my relationship with Kira's husband when he asked me why I couldn't leave Dennis. Was it because of the drinking? The getting sober together? The abortion? The children? Why can't you leave?

I didn't tell him the truth. The reason I'd never leave was simple: I love Dennis.

One day when Dennis was out of town, Chance left a message on my answering machine. "Vicki, this is Chance. Don't worry, nothing's wrong. I just wanted to see if you'd like to meet me this morning," she said. I saved the message, then replayed it, because I was interested in every nuance of her voice. Crisp and concise, like her art, it had a disarming, childlike quality that caught me off guard.

A lot went through my head, like maybe she missed Dennis so much, I was the next best thing. Or maybe something bad had happened to her, and she knew I'd once worked as a therapist and thought I might help her. Maybe she was going to tell me she was leaving Dennis, or that she was banking on my leaving him. But I think I knew that it was mere curiosity on her part. She wanted to see what I was like.

I wasn't sure what to wear. I didn't want to look matronly—I was, after all, fifteen years older than Chance—but I didn't want to look too earthy either. In the end, after many changes of clothes, I wore the white turtleneck I'd worn during the simulated-lie-detector test at Grady's office and a ragged denim skirt, just to remind her I'd once been a hippie.

When I got there, I found her in a dark corner at a table with a lamp. I had never been to this particular coffeehouse. It was a bohemian sort of place, and I wondered if she'd ever met Dennis here. I pictured him walking toward her as I was doing now. She was reading Alice Walker. *In searching for my mother's garden, I found my own* went through my mind, and I remembered that Dennis had told me that Chance's mother had suffered from manic-depression prior to her death.

Her legs were crossed Indian-style under her tiny body. Her eyes were playful but investigating. She was wearing a white turtleneck like mine.

"Have trouble deciding what to wear?" she asked, then quickly added, "So did I," and smiled. It was then that I knew what Dennis saw in her.

vicki

I ordered coffee even though I wanted a Coke, and that's when I knew how nervous I was. Whenever I feel nervous around a stranger—and, really, I rarely do—I strike a pose of transparency. I put a big card on the table, a stark fact about myself, so that the other person will squirm in my honesty.

"Who has the power in all this?" I asked her. "The men or the women? You and me, or Dennis and Kira's husband?"

She studied her mug.

"Is it about power?" she asked, and held my gaze, boldly. She wasn't a lightweight.

I tried something else. I said, "This obsession I've felt for Kira's husband, the addiction to the misery of it all, getting dragged through, or dragging myself through, all that stuff with Kira. That's not love, is it?"

I think I was fishing. I wanted her to tell me she understood because she wondered the same thing about herself in regard to Dennis.

"I don't think it's easy to understand love," she replied.

"Tell me about your family," I said. That's my other way to handle anxiety. Ask the other person about his or her family, and she'll be forced to fold.

Instead, she asked about *my* mother. I told her that my dad had taken a fall in the house and sent Mother to a neighbor's for help. She'd fallen outside and spent all night in the yard. The newspaper boy found her. I told her that my mother couldn't talk anymore, but she kept making an *s* sound. The word she wanted to say started with S.

"I wonder," I said, "if it is suicide or save or stop or shut up or salvation or shit or sweetheart."

Chance shrugged sympathetically.

"She puts her fingers to my lips as if to pull the word from *my* mouth," I went on. "I make the *s* sound, and she strains forward, like 'Come on, baby, you can say it.' "

Chance nodded.

We were quiet for a long while, and I looked at the books she was reading. I could tell that most of them were feminist in nature. She was almost a generation removed from me. I figured she was too old for Generation X but much, much too young for a baby boomer.

"One thing," she said, finally, and leaned closer to me.

I tried not to study her hands.

"I want you to understand that I do not want anybody's marriage to fall—especially not yours," she emphasized, and I let her brown eyes penetrate me, put an imprint on me.

And she reiterated, "Especially not yours."

I don't remember what else we talked about, though I was there an hour or so. I do know that I was aware of our ca-maraderie. I understood that she was melancholic like Dennis and me, and that she was probably, like me, at that very moment forming some object in her mind, sculpting a piece of horrific art from what we were feeling for one another. Which was, I'm certain, love.

living water

vicki

It is a tribute to Dennis's determination and insanity that our family arrived in San Salvador on July 19, 1997, carrying with us our personal baggage, well-drilling equipment, tools, and a lot of flush-threaded PVC pipe. Hurricane Danny had made landfall in Louisiana before turning back into the Gulf of Mexico, but the flight was smooth anyway. On the plane, Laura showed me pictures of tornados, clouds, rainbows, and halos from her *Field Guide to Weather*. One formation was called Glory.

Ashley sat on the other side of her, carrying her quiet dignity, which is far beyond that of the twelve-year-old she was then. She wanted this trip to be fruitful. She was, and is, a very serious girl.

The last time I'd been in El Salvador, we'd arrived late in the day. In the gathering dusk I saw soldiers with automatic weapons by the roadside stands and smelled the burning sugarcane fields. But now, fourteen years later, we were arriving at midday. Despite the FMLN and ARENA signs painted on the trees and telephone poles, I recognized peace. We spent the first night at a hotel in Escalón and went to church at Iglesia Bautista Emmanuel the next morning for Sunday worship. I met the pastor, Miguel Castro, and members of the congregation. This was clearly a church much like ours back home—an oddity, Baptists who supported women in the pulpit and who faced outward to the *pueblo*, rather than inward.

The next morning we headed for Usulután, with our friend and team member, Lia. We drove through the heart of the capital, down the Boulevard de Los Héroes, toward the Pan-American Highway. The air got thicker and the graffiti got dirtier as we approached San Martín.

Ashley and Laura had been to developing countries on other mission trips, but I still wondered how they were assimilating this particular poverty—the crowdedness of it all, the swarm of people and vegetables in the roadside marketplace, muted by a black veil of pollution, not to mention the insects and smoldering heat and the rainy season's mud, which was caked on tires and shoes. In the distance was Lake Ilopango and the twin volcanoes of San Vicente rising above it. A river of trash ran down one side of the ravine, and war-displaced children walked along the railroad tracks. Most of the houses were made of cardboard or plastic, pieced together with mud, bamboo, tires, rock, anything.

We passed Cojutepeque and the turnoff to Tenancingo, where Dennis had first witnessed war; San Sebastián, where they were making hammocks; San Vicente—all the towns that I'd heard him talk of over the years. On the roadside were small *tiendas*, where red meat hung like afterbirth and live chickens awaited their deaths. Sometimes we'd see painted on concrete-block walls the words EDUCACIÓN, LA SOLUCIÓN. But no matter how disconcerting the poverty, there was the ever-present bougainvillea and flame trees. All you had to do was look upward to find fruit. Oranges, coconuts, lemons, papayas, so ripe and pickable—if we only had the legs and the knowhow to climb.

"We're getting near the Lempa River," Dennis told us.

The bridge that crosses the Lempa was a phobic's nightmare. For one thing, the real bridge, over to the left, had been blown up by the guerrillas during the war. It jutted out from either side of the land, making for a surreal optical illusion. My eye wanted to make it complete, but the middle was missing.

"Rebecca's place is just to the other side," Dennis told us as we crossed the makeshift bridge and tried to stop staring at the one that had been blown up.

The Lempa River Valley wasn't like the other places I'd seen so far in Salvador. It was humid like Alabama, sultry and insect-ridden. Women were bathing in the river. The clothes they'd washed were drying on rocks. Naked babies sat in the sun. It might seem a return to the natural world, to simplicity, and to health, if it weren't for the fact that the water was polluted and carried in it the parasites that were going to infect the toddlers who splashed in it and drank from it.

I'd met Rebecca Kragh the previous Sunday at the church in the capital. Now, in the concrete-block structure that served as home, clinic, and storage area, I watched Ashley and Laura size her up. They knew she was the real thing, a doctor dressed in a man's clothes who knew how to use a machete.

A man named Juan, who worked for Iglesia Bautista Emmanuel, appeared at the door. The plan was to leave our car at Rebecca's and use the church's truck to go to Las Burras. Juan was to accompany us.

We told Rebecca goodbye.

After a mile or so, we turned onto the unpaved road to Las Burras. It was so bumpy we banged our heads against the truck ceiling over and over. We bounced and jolted forward like dummies in the seat-belt commercials. In the distance was *la montaña de mujer*, mountain of the woman, its two breasts dark against the sky. Cactus plants, cornfields, men on horseback, and more mud than you can imagine.

"We might not make it," Dennis warned us.

I couldn't imagine making it. The tires threw mud against the truck, and then into the truck, where it settled on our bare arms and jeans.

"Stop here," Juan said at a certain juncture in the dirt road—the road being nothing more than piles of rocks and pools of mud.

"This is La Barca," Dennis told us.

At the top of the hill before us was a barn, a mission of Iglesia Bautista Emmanuel, set up to help the community learn methods of reforestation and sustainable agriculture, how to recycle waste and raise chickens.

Laura's blue bandanna had slipped low on her forehead. She had started wearing it after summer camp in order to look like a counselor there named Mitch. She adjusted the bandanna and watched the sky for signs of a storm.

Ashley stared at the barn.

Juan jumped from the truck's cab and threw open a gate. "I'm going to leave you now," he said, and I felt panic crawl up my legs.

.　　.　　.

I have never liked camping. I take two or three baths a day. I'd never hike the Appalachians. I don't want to walk across America, because I might have to eat breakfast at a place that doesn't serve ice-cold Coca-Cola, which I must have every morning. I travel with my favorite pillow. Unlike Dennis, I don't want raw adventure. It's true that I liked trippy drugs back in the old days. But I used them in nice apartments with carpets, refrigerators, and friends. All this is to say that, by the time we left the barn at Barca, with Jorge in the front and a teenage boy, Raúl, in the bed of the truck, I was mildly uncomfortable. As we pushed deeper and deeper into the countryside, I stopped thinking in English. The *hombres* in their *sombreros*, riding their *caballos*, under the big *cielo*, here in the month of *julio*, were starting to shimmy in the hot sun. There was no turning back.

When we came to the San Benito River, we drove right through it. The water was almost up to the windows.

"We're crossing a river in a truck!" I wailed.

Downstream was a white horse, standing like an icon. I felt I'd dreamed all this. I had, in fact, dreamed it. When I was pregnant with Ashley, I'd dreamed of an ivory mare standing in the Gulf of Mexico.

After we crossed the river, the road became bumpier still. I prayed for safety, for a sign from God that we hadn't lost our minds. But when we tried to turn onto the final path to Las Burras, the truck refused, mired in the mud. Jorge and Raúl tried to push, but no go. I knew we weren't going to get to Las Burras to the school that needed a well. I knew we'd made a valiant effort, and then—just as I thought this—

the truck lurched forward. Raúl opened the gate, and I started crying. I cried as we passed wheat and barley fields. I cried because I thought you couldn't enter the kingdom of heaven without selling all your goods to feed the poor. I thought that a rich man trying to enter the gate was like a camel passing through the needle's eye. I didn't deserve to see the blue-and-white schoolhouse with the tin roof and the broken water pump. I didn't deserve for things to *come to pass*.

We got out of the truck and walked under a tin canopy—a family's porch. A thousand baby chicks rushed toward us in a yellow river of grace. A baby slept in a hammock. The mother was cooking tortillas over a fire, but she stopped to pull up three beat-up chairs for the girls and me to sit in. I tried making conversation in Spanish, but her accent tripped me up. I realized that rural El Salvador carries a dialect all its own, just like the rural South.

Dennis talked to a man named Luis, a village leader who had been appointed to oversee the well. Luis explained that there would be disputes if the well wasn't in a central location, accessible to all the *casas*. Dennis asked Luis to show us the best place. We followed him under a canopy of coconut trees and tangled vine, through mud so thick it felt like quicksand. When we emerged, we were staring at emaciated farm animals. And then we saw the children. They didn't smile. They knew us for the aliens that we were, in our Timberlands and Levi's. The children of Las Burras hung their heads as if shy, indignant, defeated—all at once.

The women began to gather at the place where we stood. The well wasn't even there yet, but the women were gathering anyway, as if they might, through the power of a circle, make water spring from the earth. In Las Burras, as in most developing countries, women carry water and men control. In order to make a well project work, I was aware, the village women must be consulted. They started talking to Dennis as if he were an engineer, as if he were a government authority, as if he were a physician. They were telling him their children were sick from drinking the river and that the last well had dried up after only a month.

I noticed that the children were warming up to Laura. She tore long strips of a banana leaf and started making a chain, and they gathered around her.

Ashley stood by Dennis, her T-shirt tied in a knot to let her midriff cool. Tall, substantial, elegantly lanky, she listened as the women spoke with the men; her eyes were fixed to the earth. She kept nudging Dennis. She was staring at the place where the well should go. She didn't need a wishbone stick to water-witch.

"Here," she whispered, and set a stone by her feet.

Jorge told us he was going to show us another possible site, and he navigated us back to the barn at La Barca.

"I want to go back to Las Burras," Ashley insisted.

We looked at her. She had always been willful and determined, and we didn't want to listen to the usual. We were all very dehydrated, and we hadn't eaten any lunch. I told the kids we had to try to get something down, so we sat in the barn and ate the bread and peanut butter we'd brought. We drank Gatorade and tried to get cool.

After lunch, Dennis and I started talking to Jorge about

going back to the capital. It was late, we were tired, and we were worried. But Ashley put her face in her hands.

"No," she said. "We have to go back to Las Burras," Ashley insisted.

The butterflies and flame trees were bright against the backdrop of the volcano in the distance. The fields were open, the sky blue, the land a natural wonder.

"No," I told her.

Dennis and I looked at each other.

"But it's where we're supposed to put the well. I want to put the hole in the ground!" She went to the truck and got the hand auger. "Why did you bring us here, anyway?" she demanded of Dennis. "Why did you buy this thing? Why am I here? We have to go back."

I tried to explain to her that maybe we weren't supposed to put the first well in that exact place at Las Burras. Maybe we were supposed to find another place. None of my arguments worked, and finally I said one of the worst things I've ever said to one of my children or to anyone. I looked Ashley square in the eye and said, "You're arguing with God, not with me. You're trying to manipulate fate, trying to have it your way rather than God's." She cried like I'd never seen her cry, a sad and wise weeping. She told me that I shouldn't have said what I said, that I'd regret it—which I did. She told me that all she wanted was to do the right thing. The right thing, she said, was to go back to Las Burras and put a hole where she'd set the stone. If we did this, she said, we'd have a beginning.

He who began a good work in you, will be faithful to complete it. That's from the book of Philippians. It was one of the first things I read in the Bible, as an adult, that I believed. I believed it because I was a writer.

So we got back in the truck and headed for Las Burras. Jorge didn't go. He stayed at the barn. Raúl did go. He rode in the truck bed, and I'd often glance back to see his face, his smile. We went through the gate. We didn't even get stuck in the mud this time. We parked by the house with the chicks, got the hand auger from the truck, and made our way through the thicket of bamboo, coconut, and banana trees to the place where Ashley had put the stone. I didn't know what we'd do, what we'd see after we moved the stone. But we trudged on, and when we got there, we simply lifted it from the ground, set it aside, and handed the auger to our children. They took turns, turning slowly. The women once again gathered around us. This time they didn't say a word. They just watched, pulling their children to their aprons, as my children—our children—put a hole in the ground.

In time, Ashley and Laura let us have a turn.

We didn't go deep. We didn't have to. "All you need is a beginning," as Ashley had told us.

Later on, when the rest of the mission team arrived in El Salvador, they took up where Ashley and Laura had left off, and a well now sits there, the first one we augered.

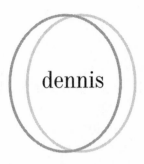

dennis

We went fifteen feet down the first day, through coarse-grained sand and silt, then eleven feet the next day, through a layer of yellow sand that was unaccountably warm to the touch and gradually more moist. By the third day, we were into a thick gray volcanic ash, wet and hot. We knew we had hit water at twenty-seven feet, but it was bound up in this steaming silt that had turned into a thick, black clay of organic sediment too hot to touch.

Our drilling slowed to inches at each attempt. Sometimes we lost more ground than we gained, but we kept on taking turns at the auger, and on the fourth day, we broke out of the black, steaming clay into a fine-grained, silty sand that was completely saturated with water.

The hole was six inches wide and forty feet deep, thirteen feet into the aquifer. We knew we had a well, but now we had to clean the water that was in it. We lowered sections of PVC pipe into the hole. The lower sections were slotted to let in the water but keep out the larger particles of sand and silt. Doug Holstein, a Seattle hydrogeologist, sifted the cuttings through wire screens to determine the appropriate particle size for a sand pack. And two Salvadorans rowed across the Lempa River and brought back the sand in their dugout canoe.

Slowly we sifted the sand into the hole, handful by handful, until it completely surrounded the pipe to a height of sixteen feet, well above the slotted sections. Then we started bailing. The bailer had a ball check valve at the bottom that let the water rush in, along with suspended sand and silt. When we lifted the bailer, the valve closed, and we could bring up the captured water and sand. We brought up forty bails in fifty minutes. The water level dropped a little, but the well recovered in less than ten minutes. So we kept on bailing, and gradually the water began to clear. The sand we'd poured in gently was acting as a final kind of filter, sorting itself by particle size and forming little bridges to keep the finest silt out.

It was like that story in the Bible when the water changes into wine, only this time it was muddy water gradually becoming so clean that there came a moment, on the afternoon of the fourth day, when we poured cups from the bailer and drank the water right out of the ground. A few brave townspeople even drank it. It tasted fine, they said, but it was a little warm. *Un poco caliente.* A joke. This water could have boiled a chicken.

When we left Las Burras, the villagers were queuing up to get water from the well. They were waving and smiling, and I was shouting in Spanish that we'd be back in December to locate sites for other wells, and back the next summer to drill them. It was a fine feeling, just to have done something practical with my hands. It wasn't like taking up snakes in church, but it was exactly what I had come for. There is, after all, a kind of spiritual ecstasy that is almost imperceptible, it runs so deep.

Last December, Vicki, Ashley, Laura, and I went back to El Salvador. We brought supplies and gifts for the children at San Martín, and we returned to Las Burras to identify sites for new wells. Rebecca Kragh wasn't in Usulután. She'd gone to Minnesota for Christmas, where she was working long hours at the local hospital earning money to support her work in El Salvador. So she didn't know at the time, and neither did we until we got there, that the pump at Las Burras had broken for a second time. The first time, in September, Rebecca and I had fixed it. Now it was broken again, a crumpling realization—time to regroup and think.

We would discover, during the course of the next few hours, that the problem was the same as it had been in September, a disconnected pump rod, but this time much farther down. Vicki, Ashley, Laura, and I would stare into the hole, fishing for the cylinder and the portion of the rod that we thought had fallen to the bottom of the well. And though we would try to improvise using cord, barbed wire, and an actual fishing hook, we wouldn't be able, that day, to bring the disconnected parts to the surface. The final repair would have to wait for Rebecca's return or for our next trip down in the spring.

But I knew we had it within us to diagnose the problem and begin the repair. We didn't have all the appropriate tools, but we did have some. Actually, the choice wasn't all that difficult. We had to give it a try.

The Salvadorans loosened and removed the nuts holding the pump to the concrete base. Ashley and Laura helped me disconnect the major parts. Then we tied the disconnected handle to the body of the pump head, to use as a lever for lifting. A Salvadoran man took one end of the handle. Vicki took the other. I pried with hammer and chisel to get the bottom of the pump free from the concrete and clear of the bolts. While I worked my way around the base of the pump, Vicki and the Salvadoran lifted. The pump didn't budge. I chiseled some more. They tried it again. Vicki stood with feet firmly set, her whole body straining against the weight of the cast-iron pump head. It was as though she were trying to curl some impossibly massive free weight, something beyond her ability but within her range of daring, something worth a monumental try, something worth failure, something worth saving. Her biceps and forceps were glistening, her calves bulging, her eyes closed, her face a sweating, contorted version of itself, as though in this instant she were looking backward down the mirrored corridor of her past at the childbirths, the losses, the pains, and the humiliating admissions of middle age. The pump head lifted a fraction, then a little more, until there was space enough to stack rocks as a wedge. Vicki and the Salvadoran lifted again, and this time the pump came free with a jolt, and I was able to disconnect the rising main and the pump rod, and Vicki and the Salvadoran could lay the superstructure aside—still heavy, but now a simple, defeated thing.

•   •   •

At the end of that week, Vicki and I were in a rental car barreling down a crowded street toward the park containing the country's most famous landmark, a statue of Jesus atop the globe. El Salvador del Mundo, the Salvadorans call it. The Saviour of the World.

I don't know what it was about the moment beyond the fact that the light was low and luminous, the crowns of the coconut palms were sharp against the sky, and the Salvadoran pedestrians, the bus passengers, the fruit vendors all seemed to be characters from a better kind of life.

"God, I haven't felt this good in years," Vicki said. And I knew exactly what she meant. As recovering alcoholics, we had often said that the worst day of sobriety was better than the best day of drinking. But this moment in the rental car—the only thing to really compare it to was the best afternoons of our drinking days, after the third or fourth one had kicked in and the world seemed dazzling and bright. It was like the beginning of a story about the two of us in the old days—on the road together, and up to no good.

It would be a while yet before I could ask Vicki's forgiveness—for the hurts I'd caused, for withholding love when it would have been so easy to give it, for using her and deceiving her and not taking her feelings seriously enough. For denying her pieces of myself, something she'd never done to me. She had always been as yielding and open as she had been on the night of Randy's party, when it was just the two of us in the world, nothing between, nowhere to go but together.

I wish I could say there was a resolution to this story of our marriage, but I can't. We are still standing, that's all. Chance and Kira's husband are not mere characters from our past. They are real people from a complicated present, and their faithfulness has placed a lien on our hearts.

To be married is to be caught in a contradiction between biology and ideas, between the certain weakness of the flesh and the weak certainty of the spirit. About the biblical imperative there is no question. The question is whether "one flesh" is just a metaphor or not. Except as manifested in the evidence of our children, Vicki and I are not the same flesh at all. We are as separate as one-celled organisms under a microscope. But our close proximity is no accident, for we wanted to be that close; we wanted to be even closer. We wanted to drop physical barriers altogether and become the same creature. We wanted the smallest part of ourselves to open up and reveal the whole. This was our passion. This was our hope. But passion is another word for suffering, and to be married is to suffer the dashing of hope.

I love Vicki. I have told her she is my shelter; she is my home. She has held our family together with a combination of contrary traits that is purely her own—silence in the face of catastrophe, action when everybody else has been struck dumb. Like me, she is reclusive, but unlike me, she has always lived for other people. That's why they can't get enough of her. Being with her is like visiting the best part of themselves, over and over. She is addictive in the only purely good sense of the word.

How does the story of our marriage end? End it as Beckett would, a friend once advised me: We can't go on. We can go on. We can't go on. We can go on. We can't go on. We can go on. We can't go on. We go on.

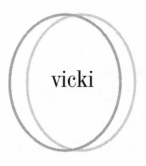

vicki

A year later, both of my parents died. My mother went first, and I knew Daddy wouldn't last long without her.

Kira's husband came to both funerals. He sat near the back, where nobody would notice but me. I was looking for him the way you look for a parent at your graduation. When I spotted him, he nodded as if to say, "I'm here."

Chance was there, too, I later learned. She signed her name in the registry book. Later, I ran my finger over her name and Kira's husband's name. Their presence at so sacred a moment seemed redemptive. It was a reminder that there are many varieties of love, some of which transcend the temporal.

When I was growing up, they taught us in Sunday school that God's love, *agape*, was the best. Agape was followed by *filial love*, which meant friendship. And then there was *eros*. The designations were like doors to me. Agape and filial led to the same room, a safe place for nice girls. Eros was in a separate closet, a Pandora's box whose contents I intuitively knew long before I opened it.

It wasn't until I was grown up that I learned there are chemical distinctions between kinds of love as well. Infatuation is caused by phenylethylamine, which must be what Kira's husband triggered in me, often by a single gesture— the paternal nod, his reticent hand moving toward a part of me. And then there is oxytocin, the "cuddle chemical" that stimulates a woman's contractions during childbirth, that causes her milk to let down when a baby cries, that makes lovemaking fluid, that begs for intimacy, connection. It's what I feel with Dennis.

Still, I wonder. I never bought the Sunday school categories, and even the laws of science don't seem to cover the complicated terrain of love.

At Mother's funeral, my dad's best friend came up to me with tears in his eyes and said, "I loved your mother, you know." I'd stake my life on the innocence of the statement, but still I wanted to beseech him: What do you mean you loved her? She was beautiful, wasn't she? Did you ever desire her? Did you imagine being married to her? Didn't you, just once in your life, want or need something from her that maybe you couldn't even name?

In Genesis, the Bible says a man is to leave his mother and father and cleave to his wife. The word means to adhere to, to cling, to hold fast an attachment to someone or something, as in bone to skin, hand to sword, the tongue to the roof of the mouth in thirst. But in English, unlike Greek or Hebrew, *cleave* carries a second, opposite meaning: to part or divide as by a cutting blow.

We cling as long as we can, but eventually every marriage ends with a cutting blow. Divorce takes half. Death takes all.

And every step of the way, we *cleave*, knowing that we are being pulled apart. Love plays us like an accordion. Together, apart, together, apart. And though we may call marriage a sacred covenant, it is also an imperfect human contract, regardless of whether fidelity prevails. Marriage is a place for realists, for soldiers, for warriors, for lovers. *To wed* is derived from the German *wetten*, which means "to bet." Marriage is, at its root, a risk, a gamble.

As we cleave, we *witness* each other in a thousand small ways—as the song goes, "every move you make, every step you take." We watch each other struggle, change, make mistakes, and ache to find God. Witnessing and being witnessed intensifies the cleaving, binds us together in a conspiracy of secrets. The secrets we know give us ways to undercut each other. My mother used to repeat to me a line of poetry that went something like *He laughed at all I dared to praise, and broke my heart in little ways*. Adultery may make the headlines, but the real betrayals are often seemingly insignificant.

If the story of my and Dennis's marriage seems peculiar, I hold it up anyway. Everybody's marriage has its own chosen architecture. And we should not be afraid of what it looks like. For after the Bible instructs a man to leave his mother and father to cleave to his wife, the rest of the verse says, "And the man and his wife were both naked, and were not ashamed." And no matter how heartbreaking marriage has been and is and will be, I want it. I wish it for my daughters, too.

For Mother's Day, a month after my own mother died, Dennis and the girls gave me a tiller. With the help of its many blades, I doubled the size of my garden. I could tear up the ground, could *beat it up*, as my grandfather used to say.

To make a garden, you disturb nature. You create an artifice. You plan to rotate crops so that you don't deplete the soil's nutrients by planting the same thing in the same place, year after year. You witness how the sun moves across the garden, so you'll know where the shadows fall. You may wonder why, in the first garden, the Tree of Knowledge was planted in the very center of the garden. You have to figure out what will grow in its shade. You hope the fruit you grow will be as good as the fruit you aren't supposed to eat, and that you won't eat from the big tree.

You may not know that the word *paradise* comes from the Persian word *pairidaeza*, meaning "walled garden," but you build a wall, a border, something to mark where the garden ends and the world at large begins. You put a border around the garden to contain it, but hope it will abundantly spill over. You prune it back, but that only makes it produce more. There is comfort in containment, but nature knows no morality. A dandelion, after all, will break concrete. It is up to you to save the garden, but you are going against the grain.

Tending the garden is hard work. And when you finally hold the harvest in your hands, you see that not everything you've grown is shaped right. There are deformities in the potatoes, a bitter cucumber among the sweet ones, a squash with end rot where it lay on the ground. You remember the seedlings that didn't make it, the ones you had to pull in order to make space for the others to grow.

It is autumn now. I like to sit outdoors, on a bench that I took from my mother's garden and put in my own. Mornings are best, when the mockingbirds make fools of themselves and the sun slants toward me. The summer crops—corn, tomatoes, okra, peppers, squash, and peas—have been harvested. I look at the land and wonder if it's too late to plant a winter garden—potatoes, turnips, carrots, and onions. I remember the first time I grubbed for a potato. The earth was moist. I went deep. I was afraid I'd find nothing there, but there were dozens of potatoes, more than we could eat.

A winter garden requires faith. All we can see of it is the foliage. What will sustain us grows beneath the ground, where nobody can see.